Tory Lee
Love
Mom & Dad

Dec 25
2000

GARDENING

THROUGH THE
YEAR

GARDENING

THROUGH THE
YEAR

A step-by-step guide to seasonal gardening tasks

Peter McHoy

SMITHMARK

This edition first published in 1995 by
SMITHMARK Publishers Inc.,
a division of US Media Holdings Inc.,
115 West 18th Street, New York, NY 10011

SMITHMARK books are available for bulk purchase for sales promotion
and premium use. For details, write or call the manager of special sales,
SMITHMARK Publishers Inc., 115 West 18th Street, New York, NY 10011

Produced by Anness Publishing Limited
Hermes House
88-89 Blackfriars Road
London SE1 8HA

ISBN 0-8317-3869-3

Publisher: Joanna Lorenz
Project Editor: Judith Simons
Designers: Patrick McLeavey & Jo Brewer
Photographer: Peter Anderson
Illustrator: Michael Shoebridge

Printed and bound in Singapore by
Star Standard Industries Pte. Ltd.

10 9 8 7

CONTENTS

INTRODUCTION

ABOVE: *Spring is a good time to plant herbaceous plants ready for summer.*

Gardening is, above all, a practical hobby. You can, of course, simply admire gardens created by others, but anyone worthy of being called a gardener enjoys the challenges of growing plants. Success does not come without effort or know-how, however, even for the experienced gardener. For the beginner, success depends largely on sound advice for all those essential tasks that lie behind the well-kept garden that we all admire. This book has been designed to provide just that kind of down-to-earth practical help that we all need from time to time.

There is no substitute for being able to see how something is

ABOVE: *Adequate feeding is one of the keys to success for container plants.*

ABOVE: *As soon as the summer display is over, replant containers for a spring display.*

done. Not only are pictures clearer than any amount of written instructions, but they reassure you that the advice is based on actual experience. With over 600 step-by-step illustrations, as well as plenty of inspirational pictures to spur you on, this book provides a dependable gardening companion which is always on hand to help: your own expert to show you how things are done, and when.

You will find this book invaluable not only because jobs are illustrated with step-by-step pictures, but also because they are arranged by season, too. If you are not sure what you should be doing now, this book will tell you *and* show you.

ABOVE: *Christmas roses are hardy, but protection will prevent mud splashes.*

The gardening season

Jobs have been arranged by seasons rather than precise weeks, as gardening is very much dependent on the weather, and precise dates can be misleading and even potentially hazardous to your plants.

You cannot garden successfully by the calendar alone. Frosts can come early in autumn or occur unexpectedly in early summer. The ground may be frozen when you would like to be planting, or too dry when you want to sow your summer seeds. Use the suggested timings as a guide, but be prepared to bring things forward or put them back to suit your own area and the particular season.

The most time-critical jobs are likely to be in spring and autumn, and when frost-tender plants are put outside or taken in. If in doubt about the best time, it is always worth making a note of when your local parks department does the job.

Winter jobs, on the other hand, are usually less time-critical and in many cases it will not matter if you move a job backwards or forwards by as much as a month. This is fortunate as it gives you the opportunity to delay a job if the weather is harsh, and to make up for lost time during those brighter spells.

LEFT: *Azaleas are popular shrubs, but they require an acid soil. You can use a simple kit to check the soil acidity.*

RIGHT: *Modern solidago hybrids are excellent border plants for late summer.*

LEFT: *Varieties of* Anemone x hybrida *and* A. hupehensis *come into their own when most border flowers are over.*

RIGHT: Sorbus aucuparia *will sometimes retain its berries into winter if birds don't eat them first.*

SPRING

*This is a time when gardeners need no encouragement.
With lengthening days, the air less chilly, and plump buds and birdsong
to stir the imagination, it is the time when gardeners cannot wait to start
propagating and planting. Early spring is a time for caution, however,
as winter seldom comes to a convenient end as spring approaches.
One of the most common causes of disappointment for novice gardeners is
sowing or planting too early – especially outdoors. Often, plants and
seeds put out several weeks later in the season overtake ones planted
earlier because they are less likely to receive a check to growth.*

OPPOSITE: *Even small spring flowers make a
strong display, like this group of narcissi,
pulmonarias, and* Anemone blanda.

ABOVE: *Tulips are among the most beautiful
spring flowers, but they look even better when
interplanted with forget-me-nots.*

EARLY SPRING

IN COLD REGIONS THE WEATHER CAN still be icy in early spring, but in mild climates you can make a start on many outdoor jobs. If sowing or planting outdoors, bear in mind that soil temperature as well as air temperature is important. Few seeds will germinate if the soil temperature is below 45°F, so use a soil thermometer to check before you sow.

JOBS IN BRIEF

The kitchen garden

- ☐ Apply manures and fertilizers where appropriate
- ☐ Plant onion sets and shallots
- ☐ Warm up the soil with cloches
- ☐ Sow early crops in cold frames or beneath cloches
- ☐ Start sowing vegetables without protection if you live in a mild area – many kinds can be sown from early spring onwards, so check the packets as some varieties are more suitable than others for early sowing
- ☐ Use horticultural fleece or floating cloches for early crops if you don't have conventional cloches
- ☐ Chit 'seed' potatoes
- ☐ Apply fertilizer to fruit bushes if they need it
- ☐ Put cloches over strawberries if you want an early crop
- ☐ Plant new strawberries

BELOW: *Plant strawberries, but make sure they are healthy and disease-free.*

The flower garden

- ☐ Finish planting bare-root trees and shrubs
- ☐ Plant container-grown shrubs
- ☐ Plant herbaceous plants
- ☐ Sow hardy annuals
- ☐ Feed and mulch beds and borders
- ☐ Plant gladioli and summer bulbs

BELOW: *Sow a new lawn when the weather is mild and moist.*

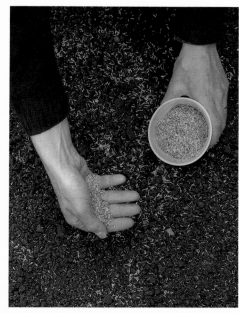

- ☐ Start mowing the lawn, but cut high initially
- ☐ Sow a new lawn or lay a lawn from turf
- ☐ Buy seeds and bulbs if not already done so
- ☐ Sow sweet peas
- ☐ Spring prune shrubs, if applicable
- ☐ Tidy up the rock garden, and apply fresh stone chippings where necessary

The greenhouse and conservatory

- ☐ Take chrysanthemum cuttings
- ☐ Start off begonia and gloxinia tubers
- ☐ Pot up pelargonium and fuchsia cuttings rooted earlier
- ☐ Pot up chrysanthemums rooted earlier

BELOW: *Pot up cuttings as soon as they are growing vigorously.*

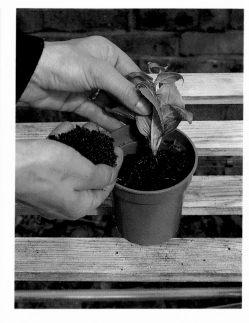

- ☐ Take dahlia cuttings
- ☐ Sow seeds of bedding plants and pot-plants
- ☐ Prick out or pot up seedlings sown earlier
- ☐ Increase ventilation on warm days
- ☐ Check plants for signs of pests and diseases, which often begin to multiply rapidly as the temperatures rise

PLANTS AT THEIR BEST

Bergenia (non-woody evergreen)
Camellia (shrub)
Chionodoxa (bulb)
Crocus (bulb)
Eranthis hyemalis (bulb)
Garrya elliptica (shrub)
Helleborus orientalis (herbaceous)
Hyacinthus (bulb)
Iris reticulata (bulb)
Magnolia stellata (shrub)
Mahonia (shrub)
Muscari armeniacum (bulb)
Primula × polyantha
(herbaceous)
Prunus cerasifera (tree)
Tulipa kaufmanniana (bulb)

ABOVE: *A* Tulipa kaufmanniana *variety.*

LEFT: Iris reticulata.

BELOW: *Chionodoxas and crocuses.*

PLANT ONION SETS

The biggest onions are usually grown from seed, but unless you can give them the dedicated care they need the results will be disappointing. Sets (small onion bulbs) are an almost foolproof way to grow onions, and you should be rewarded with a reasonable crop for very little effort.

1 Open up a shallow drill with the corner of a hoe or rake, using a garden line for a straight row. Space the sets about 6in apart.

2 Pull the soil back over the drill, but leave the tips of the onions protruding. If birds are a problem – they may try to pull the onions out by the wispy old stems – protect with netting or keep pushing the bulbs back until rooted.

PLANT SHALLOTS

Shallots are useful for pickling, but also store well for use like onions. They are almost always grown from bulbs, bought or saved from last year's crop.

1 Planted in the same way as onion sets, shallots are spaced about 6in apart, but the bulbs are larger, so the drill might have to be a little deeper. Push the bulbs into the base of the drill so that the tip is just protruding. Pull the soil back round them with a hoe or rake.

2 Shallots are useful for an early crop, and you can usually plant them outdoors in late winter, except in very cold regions. If you missed the winter planting but still want to get them growing quickly, start them off in individual pots.

3 Keep the pots in a cold frame or greenhouse until the shoots are 1–2in high. Then plant the sprouted shallots in the garden, spacing them about 6in apart.

SOW EARLY VEGETABLES OUTDOORS

Early sowing can be a gamble. If the weather is cold the seeds may rot before they germinate, and some vegetables tend to run to seed if they are subjected to cold conditions after germinating.

Concentrate early sowings on hardy crops like fava beans and early peas. Try a few short rows of a wider range of vegetables, but be prepared to resow if they don't do well.

1 Peas are best sown in multiple rows so that they can support each other, with walking space between the double or triple rows. Fava beans are also often grown in multiple rows. Open up a flat-bottomed drill about 2–3in deep.

2 Space the seeds by hand. Peas are often sown in three staggered rows, spacing the seeds about 1½in apart, but you can double this space and still get a good crop. Fava beans are sown in two rows with each seed about 9in apart.

3 Pull the soil back over the drill to cover the seeds. If the ground is dry, water well until the seedlings are through. If seed-eaters such as mice are a problem, netting or traps may be necessary.

AN EARLY START

Peas and beans germinate readily in warm soil, but are less reliable in early spring when the soil temperature fluctuates. You can be more sure of

your early peas if you start the seeds off in a greenhouse or cold frame first, then plant them out when they are growing well.

1 A length of old gutter is ideal for starting off the seeds. Block the ends and fill with soil.

2 Sow the seeds about 2–3in apart, cover, then keep warm and moist.

3 When ready to plant out, open up a shallow drill with a draw hoe, and gradually slide the peas out of the gutter and into the row.

FERTILIZE THE VEGETABLE PLOT

The vegetable plot needs regular feeding if yields are not to suffer. Unlike beds and borders in the ornamental garden, little natural recycling occurs. The crops are removed and leaves do not naturally fall and decay. Bulky organic manures do much to improve soil structure and increase the nutrient-holding capabilities of the soil, but unless you follow an intensive organic approach and apply sufficient manures and garden compost, some chemical fertilizers are necessary if you want a heavy crop.

INDIVIDUAL BOOSTERS

Throughout the growing season, certain vegetables may need boosters from specific fertilizers or quick-acting general fertilizers whenever growth seems to need encouraging. Spring cabbages often benefit from a light dressing of a nitrogenous fertilizer to stimulate the growth of fresh young leaves now that the weather is improving. Fruit crops, such as tomatoes, benefit from a high-potash feed.

1 The quickest way to apply a general fertilizer to your vegetable plot is with a wheeled spreader that you can adjust to deliver the appropriate amount. Calculate and test the delivery rate first.

2 If applying by hand, measure out the amount of fertilizer required for a square yard, so that you can visualize how much you need. Or pour it into a small container as a measure and note how full it is.

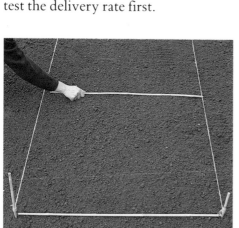

3 Mark out yard widths with strings, then use a couple of stakes to divide these into yard squares. When one square has been applied, move the back stake forward to mark out the next area.

4 Use your measure to scoop up the appropriate amount of fertilizer (use the application rates advised on the packet as a guide), then scatter it evenly. Hold the hand about 6–9in above the soil.

5 Always rake the fertilizer into the surface. This spreads it more evenly and helps it to penetrate more rapidly.

HORTICULTURAL FLEECE

Horticultural fleece is a material that a previous generation of gardeners didn't possess, but the fact that it is now widely used commercially is evidence of its usefulness. The fleece will warm up the soil rather like a cloche, and should provide protection from a degree or two of frost. It also offers protection from animals such as rabbits and pests such as caterpillars. You can use it just to start off your seeds, or as protection for a growing crop.

1 Sow your seeds then cover the area with the fleece. Anchor it down loosely with bricks or stones initially, while you secure the edges.

FLOATING CLOCHES

Other types of protective covers can also be used successfully. Some are very fine, long-lasting nets (see top), which give little frost protection but effectively keep out most animals and pests, others are perforated plastic films (see above) that let rain through and 'give' enough to rise with the growing crop.

You will have to pull them back to weed and thin. You will find that weeds thrive with the protection as well as the crops!

2 You can secure the edges with soil. Make a slit to tuck the end into, or just heap soil over the edges. Water will flow through the fleece, and it will also stretch a little as the plants grow.

3 You can buy various designs of ready-made pegs to hold the fleece in position, and these are preferable to the soil method as they make it easier to lift and replace the fleece for weeding and other cultivation tasks.

SOW HARDY ANNUALS

Hardy annuals are among the easiest plants to grow – they are undemanding of soil and are simply sown where they are to grow. Provided you thin overcrowded seedlings and give them a sunny position, the results are almost always bright and pleasing.

1 It pays to prepare the ground by clearing it of weeds, and raking the surface to a fine, crumbly structure.

2 If you are growing just for cutting, sow in rows in a spare piece of ground, but if you want to make a bright border of hardy annuals, 'draw' your design on the ground with sand and grit.

3 Use the corner of a hoe or rake to draw shallow drills, but change the direction of the drills from one block to the next to avoid a regimented appearance. Check the packet for spacing between rows.

4 Sprinkle the seeds as evenly as possible. If the weather is very dry, run water into the bottom of each drill first and allow it to soak in.

5 Write and insert a label, then cover the seeds by raking the soil back over the drills. Try not to disturb the seeds unnecessarily.

SOWING BROADCAST

Sowing in rows makes thinning and weeding much easier – especially if you don't know what the seedlings look like and find it difficult to distinguish desirable seedlings from weeds. Sometimes, however, the seeds are sown broadcast (scattered randomly) to create a more informal patch of flowers. This is particularly useful for a packet of mixed annuals, for example, where you might want to create the appearance of a wild garden.

Scatter the seeds as evenly as possible (see above), then rake them in – first in one direction and then at right angles.

6 Water thoroughly if the soil is dry and rain is not forecast. Continue to water in dry weather until the seedlings have emerged.

PLANT GLADIOLI

Gladioli are popular, and easy to grow, but their location in the flower garden needs careful thought. Grow them in rows in a spare piece of ground if you want them for cutting, but they look best planted in blocks or clusters when grown among companion plants.

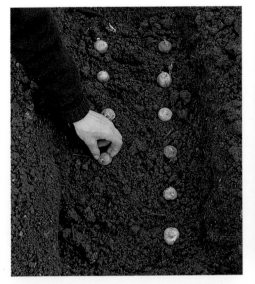

1 If you are growing gladioli for cutting rather than garden display, grow them in rows. Open up a trench as shown deep enough to cover the corms with about 3–4in of soil. Deep planting reduces the need for staking.

2 Space the corms as recommended on the packet. Planting a double row like this makes supporting easier for tall varieties. Return the soil to the trench to cover them.

OTHER BULBS TO PLANT

Most other summer-flowering bulbs, corms and tubers can be planted in the same way as gladioli, though it is too early to plant any very frost-sensitive plants as the shoots may emerge while frosts are still likely.

As a guide to planting depth, most bulbs should be covered with twice their own depth of soil. If the bulb is 1in deep, cover it with 2in of soil. As ever, there are a few exceptions to this rule.

Some tubers tend to become very dry and shrivelled after a long storage period. You can usually plump them up by soaking in water for a day before you plant, like the anemone tubers shown.

3 If planting in a border among other plants, take out a roughly circular hole, place a group of about five or seven corms in the base, and return the soil. If the ground is heavy, dig in some sand or grit before planting the corms.

4 It is easy to forget where bulbs are planted in a border, so apart from labeling, insert a few small stakes around them so that you don't accidentally hoe off the shoots before they emerge.

PLANT SHRUBS

Spring is an ideal time to plant shrubs. You can plant container-grown shrubs in any month provided the ground is not too frozen. However, spring is ideal because the soil is moist and also warm enough for new root growth to help the plant become established quickly.

1 Always clear the area of weeds, and dig out any deep-rooted perennials that will be difficult to eradicate if they grow within the root system of the shrub. Dig in plenty of garden compost or rotted manure.

2 Excavate a large hole, about twice the width of the pot or root-ball. To check the depth, place the plant in position and use a stake or stick across the hole to judge whether the shrub will be at its original depth in the soil.

3 If the roots are dry, water the plant thoroughly then leave for an hour. If roots are wound tightly around the inside of the pot, tease out some of the fine ones to encourage them to grow out into the soil.

4 Place the root-ball in the hole and check that the soil will be level with the potting soil in the root-ball. Return the soil, and firm it well to eliminate large air pockets.

5 To get your shrubs off to a good start, apply a general garden fertilizer at the recommended rate and sprinkle around the plant. Keep away from the stem. Water well.

6 'Balled' or 'root-wrapped' shrubs are sold with their roots wrapped in burlap or a plastic material. Check the depth as before.

7 When the plant is in position, untie the wrapper and slide it out of the hole. Avoid disturbing the ball of soil around the roots.

8 Replace the soil, and firm well to eliminate large pockets of air. Apply fertilizer and water as described for container-grown plants.

9 It is worth mulching the ground after planting. It will conserve moisture and some mulches, such as chipped bark, look attractive too.

PLANT HERBACEOUS PLANTS

Herbaceous border plants can be planted at any time from containers, but most gardeners prefer to get them planted in spring so that they contribute to the summer show.

If you buy plants by mail order they may arrive as small root-wrapped plants, and these should be planted before the new shoots emerge, or are still very short.

ROOT-WRAPPED HERBACEOUS PLANTS

If your herbaceous plants are root-wrapped, keep them in a cool, shady place until you are ready to plant. Make sure that the plants are kept moist at all times.

Remove the wrapping only just before you are ready to plant. Spread the roots out widely within the planting hole before returning the soil.

Root-wrapped plants are more vulnerable than container-grown plants until they become established, so take extra care and keep them well watered.

1 If planting a border, lay the plants out first so that you can visualize the result (don't forget to allow for growth!). It is easier to move them around at this stage, before planting.

2 Water the plants about an hour before you start, and knock them out of their pots only when you are ready to plant.

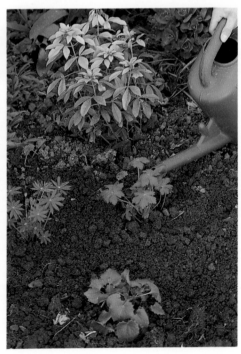

3 Ensure the ground is clear of weeds before planting, and work methodically from the back of the border or from one end. Most can be planted with a trowel but you may need a spade for large plants.

4 Return the soil, making sure that the plant is at its original depth, and firm well to eliminate any large pockets of air that could cause the roots to dry out.

5 Water the plants thoroughly unless the weather is wet or heavy rain is forecast.

SOW A NEW LAWN

The advantage of a lawn from seed is that it is usually less expensive than turf and you can choose the grass seed mixture. Some turf specialists also offer seed mixtures to suit your specific requirements, but these can be expensive.

Thorough ground preparation is essential for a quality lawn, and this should start several weeks before sowing. If you don't have time to prepare the ground properly this spring, wait and sow in the autumn instead.

1 Dig the ground thoroughly, and make every effort to eliminate difficult or deep-rooted perennial weeds. Then rake the soil level. Use pegs marked with lines drawn 2in down from the top as a guide, having checked with a spirit-level on a straight-edge that the pegs are level.

2 Allow the soil to settle for a week, then consolidate it further by treading it evenly to remove large air pockets. The best way to do this is to shuffle your feet over the area, first in one direction then at right angles.

3 Rake the consolidated soil to produce a fine crumbly structure suitable for sowing seeds. If you can, leave the area for a couple of weeks to allow weed seeds to germinate. Hoe them off or use a weedkiller that leaves the ground safe for replanting within days.

4 Use string to divide the area into yard strips, and divide these into yard lengths with stakes. Move the stakes along the strips as you sow.

5 Use a small container that holds enough seed for a square yard (make a mark on it if the amount only partly fills the container). Scatter the seeds as evenly as possible with a sweeping motion of the hand.

6 If you have to sow a large area it might be worth renting a seed/ fertilizer distributor that you can simply wheel over the area. Always check the delivery rate over sheets of paper or plastic first. Lightly rake the seed into the surface. Use a water sprinkler if necessary to keep the soil moist until the seeds germinate.

LAY A LAWN FROM TURF

Turf provides the best method of creating a lawn quickly – you can use it within months – and soil preparation is a little less demanding. You will usually find that it is a more expensive option than seed, but many gardeners are happy to pay a premium for the convenience.

1 Dig and consolidate the soil as described for seed, but there is no need to leave it for a few weeks to allow weed seeds to germinate – the turf will prevent them from germinating. Start by laying the turf along a straight edge.

2 Use a plank to stand on while you lay the next row, as this will help to distribute your weight. Stagger the joints between rows to create a bond like brickwork. If using turf as a long roll there will be fewer joints. Make sure these do not align.

3 Tamp down each row of turf (you can use the head of a rake as shown), then roll the plank forwards to lay the next row.

4 Brush sieved sandy soil, or a mixture of peat and sand, into the joints. This will help to bind the turves together.

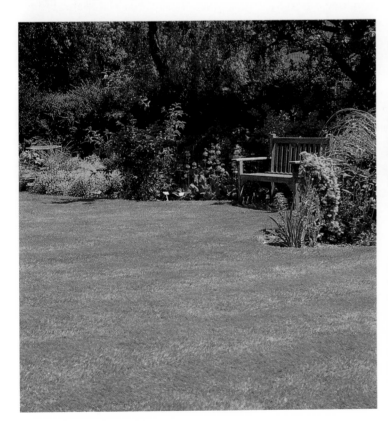

ABOVE: *A lawn can create a sense of space and is often the central part of the garden. Here an informal shape creates a natural look.*

5 Shape edges when the lawn is laid. Lay a hose or rope to form the shape for a curved edge, or use a straight-edged piece of wood for a straight-edge, and trim with a half-moon edger.

SPRING PRUNE SHRUBS

Only prune shrubs that you know require spring pruning, otherwise you may cut out the shoots that will bear this year's flowers. Advice is given below for some popular shrubs that need spring pruning, but if in doubt about others consult an encyclopedia that gives pruning information.

1 Prune shrubs grown for colored winter stems shortly before new growth starts. These include *Cornus alba* and *Cornus stolonifera* varieties and *Salix alba* 'Chermesina' (syn. 'Britzensis'). Only prune plants that have been established for a few years.

2 Cut back all the stems to an outward-facing bud about 2in from the ground or stump of old, hard wood.

3 Although the pruning seems drastic, new shoots will soon appear and by next winter will make a splendid sight. Prune annually if you feed and mulch the plants, otherwise every second spring.

4 Some popular gray-leaved shrubs, such as *Santolina chamaecyparissus* and *Helichrysum angustifolium*, need regular pruning if they are to remain neat and compact.

5 If you prune the plant regularly from a young age, prune back close to the base to a point where you can see new shoots developing. This may be as low as 4in from the ground on some plants, but on old, woody plants you will have to leave a taller framework of woody shoots.

6 The plant will look bare and sparse after pruning, but within a month should be well clothed again.

7 *Buddleia davidii* produces its flowers at the tops of tall, lanky stems if left unpruned. Each spring, cut back all the shoots to within about two buds of the previous year's growth, close to the old stump.

8 Again, this type of pruning looks drastic but it will greatly enhance the look of the plant later in the year.

A few shrubs related to the blackberry are grown for their white winter stems. The shoots arise from ground level like raspberry canes, and these are best cut back every year. Cut all the stems off close to the ground. New shoots will soon grow and the plant will be just as attractive next winter.

PRUNE ROSES

Trials have shown that you can achieve very good results from hybrid tea (large-flowered) and floribunda (cluster-flowered) roses simply by cutting them roughly to an even height with pruners, or even a hedgetrimmer, without worrying about the detailed pruning shown here. The conventional method is still practiced by most rose enthusiasts, however. Don't worry if you make one or two wrong cuts – the roses will probably still bloom prolifically.

1 Moderate pruning is the most appropriate for established hybrid tea roses. Cut back the stems by about half, to an outward-facing bud to keep the center of the bush open.

2 You can treat floribundas in the same way, but if you prune some shoots severely and others lightly, flowering may be spread over a longer period. Prune the oldest shoots back close to the base, those that grew last year by about a third only.

3 Whichever type of rose you are pruning, cut back any dead or diseased shoots to healthy wood.

START OFF BEGONIA AND GLOXINIA TUBERS

Tuberous-rooted begonias can be grown as pot-plants or in the garden, but wherever they are destined it is well worth starting them into growth now in the greenhouse. This way you will have well-developed plants to put in the garden that will flower much earlier than if the tubers were planted directly into the soil.

Gloxinias, which are suited to a warm porch, or for the home or greenhouse, should also be started into growth now.

1 If you are growing your begonias as pot-plants, start them off in small pots to save space in the early stages. Loosely fill the pots with a peat-based or peat-substitute mixture intended for seeds or cuttings.

2 If the tubers have small shoots it will be obvious which is the top, otherwise look for the side with a slight hollow and keep this upwards. Just press the tuber into the soil mix. Keep in a warm, light place, ideally in a greenhouse.

3 If the begonias are intended for outdoors, perhaps in containers or baskets, start them off in trays instead of pots as this will save space.

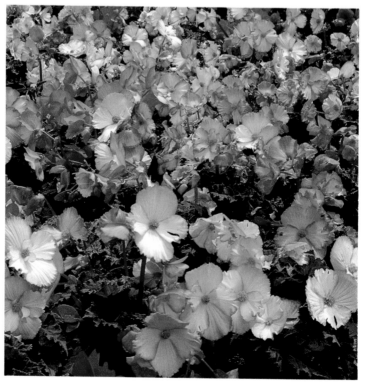

LEFT: 'Pin-up' is an outstanding single tuberous-rooted begonia that can be raised from seed to flower in its first year or overwintered as a dry tuber.

4 Gloxinia tubers are started into growth in the same way, but as they will be grown as pot-plants you may prefer to plant them in their final 5–6in pots. The 'hairy' side (the remains of old roots) is the one to press into the soil mix.

POT UP AND POT ON CUTTINGS

Pot up cuttings, such as those of pelargoniums and fuchsias, to ensure that their growth rate is not checked. With warmer temperatures they will now be growing vigorously.

1 Pot up the cuttings as soon as they have formed strong root growth. Use a 3–4in pot and a potting mixture suitable for young plants. Water thoroughly, then keep out of direct sunlight for a couple of days while they recover from the root disturbance.

2 Cuttings that rooted earlier and have already been potted up for a month or more may need moving into larger pots. Check that the roots have filled the potting mixture before you transfer them. If the mixture has lots of white roots, pot on into a larger size.

3 Use a pot a couple of sizes larger, and trickle the same kind of potting mix around the root-ball. Firm well to remove air pockets, and water thoroughly.

ENCOURAGE BUSHY FUCHSIAS

Bush-shaped fuchsias respond well to early 'pruning' and training. You can start as soon as the cuttings have three pairs of leaves.

1 Pinch out the growing tip of your fuchsia cuttings once three pairs of leaves have formed, if you want a bushy shape.

2 New shoots will form after a few weeks, but for really bushy plants pinch out the tips of these sideshoots too. Repeat this process several times throughout spring to encourage well-shaped bushy plants.

SAVING SPACE IN THE GREENHOUSE

Greenhouse space is often a problem at this time of year. If you are growing cuttings for the garden rather than as pot-plants, keep the young plants in small pots rather than potting them on into larger ones. To avoid a check to growth, however, you must feed the young plants regularly to avoid starvation. Move them to a frost-free cold frame as soon as it is warm enough to do so, and allow plenty of space between the plants so that the leaves are not overcrowded.

PRICK OUT SEEDLINGS

Prick out seedlings as soon as they are large enough to handle. If you leave them in their original trays or pots too long, they will quickly become overcrowded and difficult to separate without damage. Some plants are best pricked out into individual pots (see opposite), but this takes up a lot of space and soil mix, so most bedding plants are pricked out into trays. Instead of pricking out into trays, you can use a modular or cell system, like the one shown here, where each plant has its own pocket of soil, separated from the others. The benefit of this method is that there will be less root disturbance when the plants are eventually put into the garden.

1 Choose a module that suits the size of plant. A small seedling such as ageratum or fibrous-rooted begonia will not need such a large cell as, say, a dahlia. Fill the individual cells loosely with a potting mixture suitable for seedlings.

2 Strike the soil mix off level with a straight-edge, but do not compress it. It will settle lower in the cells once the seedlings have been inserted and watered.

3 Loosen the seedlings in the tray or pot you are pricking out from, and if possible lift them one at a time by their seed leaves. These are the first ones to open, and they are usually smaller and a different shape to the true leaves.

4 Use a tool designed for the purpose, or improvise with something like a pencil or plant label, to make a hole large enough to take the roots with as little bending or disturbance as possible.

5 Gently firm the soil mix around the roots, being careful not to press too hard. Water thoroughly, then keep the plants out of direct sunlight for a couple of days.

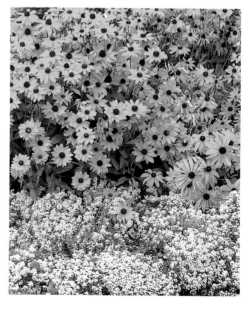

ABOVE: *The white alyssum and bright golden annual rudbeckias are among many colorful annuals to be pricked out now.*

PRICK OUT INTO POTS

Some plants, such as bedding pelargoniums and pot-plants for the greenhouse and home, are best pricked out into individual pots rather than trays or even modules.

1 Fill small pots with potting mixture and firm it lightly, using the base of another pot.

2 Loosen the soil mix with a small dibber or transplanting tool. Hold the seedling by its leaves, not the stem.

3 Make a small hole in the center of the pot, deep enough to take the roots without damage.

4 While still holding the seedling by a leaf, very gently firm the potting mixture around the roots, using a small dibber or a finger. Don't press too hard as watering will also settle the mixture around the roots.

5 Water carefully so that the potting mixture is settled around the roots without washing the plant out. Keep the seedlings in a warm, humid place out of direct sunlight for a few days.

6 Writing labels for individual pots is tedious and you probably won't want to do it, yet confusion later is highly probable if you have lots of pots containing different varieties. Group individual varieties into trays, and use just one label.

PRICKING OUT TINY SEEDLINGS

Seedlings are almost always pricked out individually, but there are a few special cases when more than a single seedling is used. Lobelia seedlings are tiny, and individual plants not very substantial, so many gardeners prick out a small group of seedlings together, as shown. Prick out about five or six plants at a time, though the number is not critical. Pricking out tiny seedlings in small groups like this also makes the job much quicker and easier, but it is only recommended for certain plants.

By the time these grow into seedlings large enough to plant out they look like one substantial plant.

MID SPRING

FOR MANY GARDENERS MID SPRING IS the most exciting as well as the busiest time of the year. The garden looks colorful again by this time, seedlings and cuttings are growing fast, and outdoor sowing and planting can begin in earnest. This is often a time when priorities have to be decided if it isn't possible to keep up with all those urgent jobs. If you don't know whether something can wait, check in the Jobs In Brief notes for late spring: this may enable you to decide what can be delayed. Plants sown or planted in late spring often catch up with those sown a month earlier if the weather happens to be unseasonably cold.

JOBS IN BRIEF

The kitchen garden

- ☐ Apply manures and fertilizers where appropriate
- ☐ Plant onion sets
- ☐ Plant asparagus crowns
- ☐ Continue to sow in cold frames or beneath cloches for earlier crops
- ☐ Start sowing vegetables without protection – many kinds can be sown from mid spring onwards, so check the packets
- ☐ Use horticultural fleece or floating cloches for early crops if you don't have conventional cloches
- ☐ Plant potatoes
- ☐ Plant out vegetable seedlings such as cabbages
- ☐ Apply fertilizer to fruit bushes if they need it
- ☐ Put cloches over strawberries if you want an early crop
- ☐ Plant new strawberries

BELOW: *Plant cabbage and cauliflower plants when the weather is moist and mild.*

The flower garden

- ☐ Plant and stock the pond
- ☐ Divide over-large pond plants
- ☐ Plant container-grown shrubs
- ☐ Plant herbaceous plants
- ☐ Stake herbaceous plants
- ☐ Sow hardy annuals
- ☐ Feed and mulch beds and borders

BELOW: *Aquatics are best planted before growth is advanced.*

- ☐ Plant a hedge
- ☐ Plant gladioli and summer bulbs
- ☐ Mow the lawn regularly from now on
- ☐ Make a new lawn from seed or turf
- ☐ Buy seeds and bulbs if not already done so
- ☐ Plant out sweet peas raised in pots
- ☐ Sow sweet peas where they are to flower
- ☐ Plant ranunculus tubers

The greenhouse and conservatory

- ☐ Sow tender vegetables such as outdoor tomatoes and runner beans to plant out later, and cucumbers for the greenhouse
- ☐ Start begonia and gloxinia tubers into growth
- ☐ Pot up pelargonium and fuchsia cuttings rooted earlier
- ☐ Pot up or pot on into larger pots chrysanthemums rooted earlier
- ☐ Take dahlia cuttings
- ☐ Sow seeds of bedding plants and pot-plants
- ☐ Prick out or pot up seedlings sown earlier
- ☐ Take leaf cuttings of saintpaulias and streptocarpus

BELOW: *Softwood cuttings of many shrubs can be taken now, including fuchsias.*

PLANTS AT THEIR BEST

Amelanchier (shrub/tree)
Bergenia (non-woody evergreen)
Cytisus, various (shrub)
Dicentra (herbaceous)
Doronicum (herbaceous)
Forsythia (shrub)
Helleborus orientalis (herbaceous)
Hyacinthus (bulb)
Magnolia × soulangiana (tree)
Magnolia stellata (shrub)
Mahonia, various (shrub)
Muscari armeniacum (bulb)
Narcissus (bulb)
Primula × polyantha (herbaceous)
Prunus 'Kwanzan' (tree)
Pulsatilla vulgaris (rock plant)
Rhododendron, various (shrub)
Ribes sanguineum (shrub)
Saxifraga, various (rock plant)
Tulipa, various (bulb)

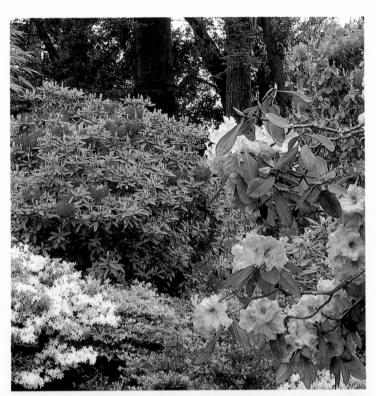

LEFT: *Rhododendrons come in many sizes and colors. Most grow tall, but some are compact enough for a small garden.*

BELOW: *Aubrietas and saxifragas can always be relied upon for a colorful display, set off here by green bergenia and juniper foliage.*

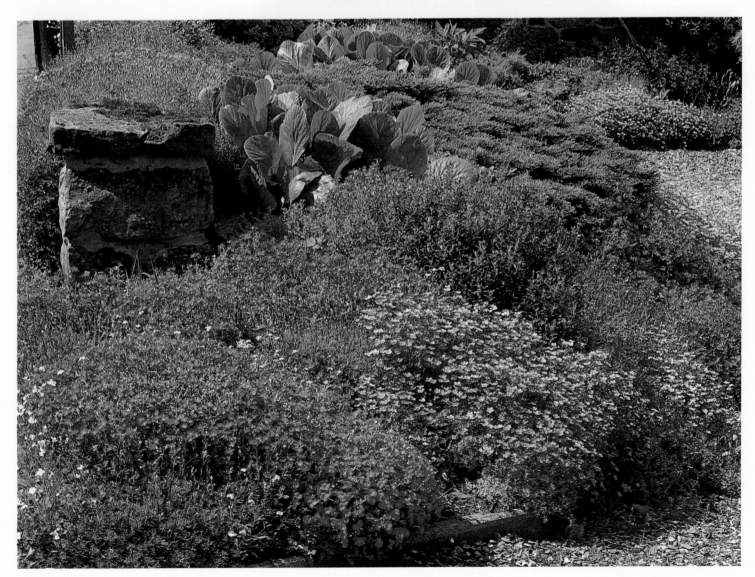

SOW MAINCROP VEGETABLES OUTDOORS

Vegetable sowing begins in earnest now, with crops like beets, spinach beet, summer cabbages, salad and pickling onions, parsnips and turnips, as well as further sowings of lettuces, peas, radishes, spinach, carrots and cauliflowers. Dwarf beans can be sown in mild areas.

1 Break the soil down into a fine crumbly structure, and level with a rake before sowing.

2 Heavy soils may be difficult to break down into a fine structure with the rake, especially if the soil is dry. Treading on the largest lumps usually helps to break them down.

3 Once the soil is reasonably fine, rake it level, and remove any large stones at the same time.

4 Most vegetables grown in rows, such as beets and carrots, are best sown in drills. Always use a garden line to make sure the drills – and therefore the rows – are straight.

5 Open up a shallow drill with the corner of a hoe or rake. Always refer to the seed packet for the recommended depth.

6 Flood the drills with water a few minutes before sowing if the weather is dry. Do it before sowing rather than after so that the seeds are not washed away or into clumps.

7 Sprinkle the seeds thinly and evenly along the drill. Do this carefully now and you will save time later when you would have to thin the seedlings if they come up too quickly.

8 Remove the garden line, then use your feet to shuffle the excavated soil back into the drills as you walk along the row. This technique is easy to master.

9 Use a rake to return soil to the drills if you find it easier, but rake in the direction of the row and not across it, otherwise you might spread the seeds and produce an uneven row.

FLUID SOWING

Fluid sowing is a technique some gardeners use to get the more difficult seeds off to a flying start. Parsnips, early carrots, onions and parsley are among the produce sometimes sown this way.

1 Sow the seeds thickly on damp paper towel, and keep in a warm place to germinate. Make sure that they remain moist, and check daily to monitor germination.

2 Once the roots emerge, and before the leaves open, wash the seeds into a sieve and mix them into prepared wallpaper paste (no fungicide) or a special sowing gel.

BELOW: *Carrots benefit from even sowing. The onions are to deter carrot fly!*

3 Open up the drill in the normal way, and to the usual depth.

4 Fill a plastic bag with the paste and cut off one corner (rather like an icing bag). Don't make the hole too large. Twist the top of the bag to prevent the paste oozing out, then move along the row as you squeeze out the seeds in the paste.

USING PREPARED SOWING STRIPS

From time to time strips of pre-sown seeds, embedded in a degradable material, may be available. These are an expensive way to buy seeds, but save much time and energy normally spent on spacing and thinning.

Open up a drill as advised and place the strip on edge in the drill. Return the soil to the drill, and keep the ground moist.

Because the seeds receive protection from the material in which they are embedded, and this sometimes also contains nutrients to give the seedlings a boost, you may find it an easy way to achieve a row of well-spaced seedlings.

PLANT POTATOES

It is safe to plant potatoes in most areas, as it will take several weeks before the frost-sensitive shoots emerge from the soil, and these can be protected by earthing up the plants. In cold areas, however, it is best to chit your potatoes (see below) and delay planting for a couple of weeks. The use of cloches, floating cloches or fleece is wise in areas where frost is still likely.

1 Use a draw hoe, spade or a rake head to make wide flat-bottomed or V-shaped drills about 4–5in deep. Space the rows about 17in apart for early varieties, 2¼ft for second earlys, and 2½ft for the maincrop.

2 Space the tubers about 12–18in apart in the rows. Make sure that the shoots or 'eyes' (buds about to grow into shoots) are facing upwards. For larger tubers, leave only about three sprouts per plant and rub the others off.

CHITTING POTATO TUBERS

Chitting simply means encouraging the potato tubers to sprout before planting. The kind of long shoots that appear when potatoes have been stored in the dark for some time are no use – the shoots must be short and sturdy. Place the tubers in a tray in a light position, perhaps by a window, where there is no risk of frost.

Chitting is useful if you want the tubers to get off to a quick start, as they will usually be through the ground a week or two before unchitted tubers.

3 Cover the tubers by pulling the excavated soil back into the drill.

4 If you don't want the effort of earthing up your potatoes, plant under a black plastic sheet. Bury the edges in slits in the soil and cover with soil to anchor the sheet.

5 Make cross-shaped slits in the plastic with a knife where each tuber is to be planted.

6 Plant through the slit, using a trowel. Make sure that the tuber is covered with 1–2in of soil. The shoots will find their way through the slits.

PLANT CABBAGES AND CAULIFLOWERS

Cabbages and cauliflowers are not normally sown in their final positions, but started off in seed beds, or sown in late winter and spring in pots or modules in the greenhouse, then transplanted to their growing positions. Buy young plants if you forgot to sow your own.

1 If you have your own seedlings to transplant into the vegetable patch – perhaps growing in a cold frame – water thoroughly an hour before you lift them if the soil is dry.

2 Loosen the soil with a fork or trowel. It is best to lift each one individually with a trowel if possible, but if they have not been thinned sufficiently this may be difficult.

3 Plant with a trowel and firm the soil well. A convenient way to firm soil around the roots is to insert the blade of the trowel about 2in away from the plant and press it firmly towards the roots.

4 You can also firm the soil with the handle of the trowel if you don't want to use your hands, but this is not a good idea if the soil is wet as it will dirty the handle. Always water in thoroughly after transplanting.

5 Cabbage and cauliflower seedlings are often raised in modules so that the plants receive less of a shock when transplanted. Many modules are designed so that you can remove the plant by squeezing the base while gently pulling the plant at the top.

PROTECTION FOR EARLY STRAWBERRIES

Strawberries do not need protection from frost, but cloches will bring the crop on earlier and will also help to keep it clean and protect it from birds and other animals.

Cover the plants as soon as possible, but remember to leave access for pollinating insects when the plants are in flower. Most cloches have a system of ventilation that can be used for this on warm days. With polyethylene tunnel cloches, lift the material along one side to allow for pollination.

ABOVE: *Space cabbages as advised on the packet, as size varies.*

PLANT WATERLILIES

This is a good time to plant your pond, whether establishing a new one or just adding new plants to an old one. Waterlilies are likely to be much more expensive than the aquatic plants that you plant around the margins of the pool, so it is worth taking special care.

1 Planting baskets are usually used for plants that grow around the edge of a pond, but for deep-water plants like waterlilies a washing-up bowl is ideal. Use a heavy soil that is not too rich in nutrients, available from aquatic specialists.

2 Never add ordinary fertilizers to the soil, as these are likely to encourage a proliferation of algae that will turn the water green. Use a special slow-release fertilizer, preferably one sold specifically for aquatic plants.

USING OXYGENATING PLANTS

Many oxygenating plants, such as elodea, remain below the surface and have little visual appeal. These are used because they are efficient at releasing oxygen into the water, which helps to keep it healthy for fish and wildlife.

Some oxygenating plants are sold as cuttings bundled together, perhaps weighted so that they sink. Just push these into a container of soil and they will soon root.

Some of the more decorative types, such as myriophyllums, which have a feathery growth above the water, are best planted in baskets like marginal aquatics.

3 Remove the waterlily from its container, and plant in the bowl at its original depth.

4 Add a layer of gravel to reduce the chance of fish disturbing the soil. Gravel also helps to keep the soil in place when the container is lowered into the water.

5 Flood the bowl with water and let it stand for a while. This will reduce the chances of the water becoming muddy when you place the bowl in the pond.

6 Place the bowl in a shallow part of the pond initially, especially if new leaves are just developing. Then push it into deeper water a week or two later.

PLANT MARGINAL AQUATICS

There is nothing marginal about the appeal of most plants that come under this description – the term merely indicates that they are planted in shallower water at the margins of the pool. Most ponds are designed with a shelf on which you can grow marginal plants, most conveniently in baskets sold for the purpose, or you can stand the plants on bricks or slabs.

INTRODUCING FISH

Never place fish directly into the pond. First acclimatize them by floating the plastic bag that you transported them in on the surface of the water for an hour, as shown. This will allow the water temperatures to equalize gradually, after which the fish can be allowed to swim out of the bag.

1 Fill a basket sold for marginal plants with garden soil that is not too rich in nutrients, or buy an aquatic soil mix. Liners are sold to prevent the soil falling through the open sides of the basket.

2 Remove the plant from its container and plant it in the basket at its original depth, using a trowel to add or remove soil as necessary. Firm it in well.

ABOVE: *Always choose waterlily varieties to suit the size of the pond. Some are suitable for a small pool, others demand a lot of space.*

3 Cover with gravel to help keep the soil in place when you place the container in the pond, and to minimize disturbance by fish.

4 Water first to moisten the soil if it is dry, then carefully place on the shelf at the edge of the pool so that the container is covered by 1–2in of water.

PLANT OR SOW SWEET PEAS

Sweet peas sown in the autumn and overwintered in a cold frame, or sown in a greenhouse in mid or late winter, will have made sturdy plants ready to be put out, but it is not too late to sow now – indoors or out – for a late summer display. To spread the period over which you can enjoy sweet peas, it is a good idea to sow at different times.

1 Insert the supports before you plant. For the best blooms, produced on long, straight stems, the cordon system is best, but it is very labor-intensive. Insert T-shaped posts at each end of the double row. Stretch wires between the cross-pieces and secure 7ft stakes to these at 9in intervals, sloping them slightly inwards.

2 For general garden display and a mass of flowers, a tepee of stakes is more satisfactory. Incline the stakes inwards and tie at the top, or use a purchased stake holder.

3 Wire or plastic netting fixed to stakes to form a circular tower is another efficient way to support tall sweet peas for general garden decoration at the back of a border.

4 Remove a hole, large enough to take the root-ball with minimal disturbance, at the base of each stake, or about 9in apart.

5 Sweet pea plants are sometimes sold with a cluster of seedlings in one pot. Always separate these and plant individually. Spread the roots out, cover, then water thoroughly.

6 Support the plants from an early stage. They can be wound in and out of netting, or attached to stakes with string or metal split rings.

7 If sowing directly into the soil, sow two or three seeds at each position, and thin to one later if more germinate.

STAKE BORDER PLANTS

Some border plants are prone to wind damage, and sometimes a potentially beautiful plant is flattened or broken by the weather. Early staking means that the plants will usually grow through or over the support, which will then become almost invisible.

1 Ready-made supports like this are very efficient at supporting border plants that are not very tall but have a mass of tallish floppy or fragile flowering stems.

2 Ready-made supports that link together as shown are useful where you have clumps of varying sizes to support. They can be linked together to suit the individual plant.

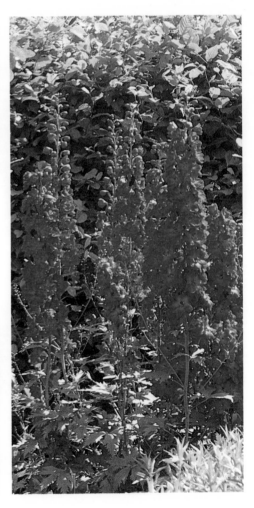

ABOVE: *Tall garden stakes are an efficient way to support plants with very tall flowering spikes that are vulnerable to wind damage, such as delphiniums. Insert individual stakes at an early stage, and tie the spike to it loosely as it grows.*

3 Twiggy sticks pushed into the ground among and around the plant can be very effective. They may look a little unsightly initially, but once the plant grows you probably won't notice them.

4 Short stakes can be used to support plants such as carnations. If you use a stout stake, loop string or twine around it and the plant. Use thinner split stakes to keep individual flower stems or groups of stems upright.

TAKE SOFTWOOD CUTTINGS

Softwood cuttings, which are taken from the new shoots produced this year, root quickly and easily, and you can multiply many of your plants this way. The list below suggests a selection of some of the more popular garden plants you can propagate in this way.

1 The exact length of a softwood cutting depends on the plant, and some gardeners prefer variations of the basic technique, but typically the stem is cut off below the third or fourth leaf or pairs of leaves.

2 Trim or pull off the lowest pair of leaves (if the plant has scale-like stipules, such as on a pelargonium, pull off these as well). Trim the base of the stem with a sharp knife, cutting just below a leaf joint.

PLANTS TO GROW FROM SOFTWOOD CUTTINGS

The following are just some of the popular plants that can be propagated from softwood cuttings taken now, but there are many more to try. It is always worth experimenting if there is a plant that you want to propagate but are not sure if softwood cuttings are suitable. The chances are that some will root.

Caryopteris
Clematis
Forsythia
Fuchsia
Helichrysum
Kolkwitzia
Lavandula
Pelargonium
Salvia (shrubby types)

3 Dip the end of the cutting into a rooting hormone for speedier rooting, although many softwood cuttings root easily without this aid. Most rooting powders contain a fungicide, however, and this also helps to prevent rotting.

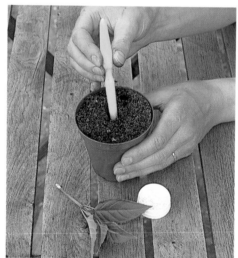

4 Make a hole with a dibber or pencil, then insert the cutting and firm the rooting mixture gently around it. Do not force the cutting in as this may damage it. If you have a lot of cuttings, insert several around the edge of each pot – but don't let the leaves touch.

5 Water and place in a propagator. If you do not have a propagator, enclose the cuttings in a plastic bag secured with a twist-tie or elastic band. High humidity is very important for softwood cuttings. Make sure that the leaves are not in contact with the bag.

PLANT A HANGING BASKET

The best hanging baskets are those planted with fairly small plants that are then grown on in a light, frost-free place until it is safe to put them outdoors – perhaps in late spring or early summer. A greenhouse is ideal, but you might also be able to use an enclosed or protected porch. Giving the baskets protection for a few weeks enables the plants to recover from the transplanting before they have to contend with the winds and drier soil and air outdoors.

1 Stand the basket on a large pot or a bucket to keep it stable while planting. Use a wire basket if you want a traditional display with plenty of plants cascading from the sides as well as the top.

2 Water-absorbing crystals can be added to the potting mixture to act as a buffer if you are occasionally forgetful about watering your plants. However, they are no substitute for regular, daily watering during dry and hot weather.

3 You can use ready-made liners and make slits for planting, but if making a traditional basket, line it with moss to the level of the first row of plants. Fill the basket with the potting mixture up to that level, then insert the plants.

4 Add more moss and potting mix and repeat until just below the rim. Use a bold plant for the center. It may be necessary to remove a little of the potting soil from the root-ball if the plant has been in a large pot.

5 Finally, fill in with plants around the edges. Encourage cascading plants to trail quickly and effectively by planting the root-ball at a slight angle so that the plant tilts slightly towards the edge.

6 Water thoroughly and keep in a warm, sheltered place until the plants are well established. If you do not have hanging facilities in the greenhouse, keep the basket on the support used while planting it.

SOW TENDER VEGETABLES

Mid spring is a good time to sow frost-tender vegetables in most areas. If they are sown too early they may be ready to plant out too soon, and they will start to suffer if they are kept in small containers for too long. Vegetables sown now should be ready for planting outdoors after a few weeks of growth in warmth followed by a week or so of acclimatization in a cold frame. In reasonably warm climates all the vegetables mentioned here can be sown outside once the risk of frost has passed. It is only worth sowing indoors if you want an early crop.

1 Sow runner beans about six to eight weeks before the last frost is likely. Fill a 6–8in pot with a sowing mixture to within 1in of the rim. Put three seeds in the pot, cover with about 2in of the sowing mixture, and water.

2 Keep the pots in a warm place, and give them good light as soon as the seeds germinate. If all the seeds germinate, pull out the surplus to leave just one or two seedlings.

3 Outdoor and greenhouse cucumbers can be sown now. Use small pots and fill with a seed-sowing mixture to within 1in of the rim. Position two or three seeds in each, placing them on their narrow edge, cover with soil mix, and water.

4 Keep the pots moist and warm until the seeds germinate. If more than one germinates, thin them at an early stage to leave just one seedling in each pot.

5 Squash and zucchini can also be started off in pots. Treat like cucumbers, but as the seeds are larger use a bigger pot and plant them about 1in deep.

6 Corn is best raised in pots to plant out later, except in very mild regions. You can use ordinary pots, but many gardeners prefer to use peat pots. The roots will grow through these once they are planted out. Peat pots are easier to manage if they are stood in a seed tray lined with a piece of capillary matting.

TAKE LEAF CUTTINGS

Some houseplants – such as saintpaulias and streptocarpus – root readily from various types of leaf cuttings. Two methods are shown here.

Although you can root them at almost any time of the year, spring is a good time as the young plants will grow quickly.

1 The kind of cuttings taken from saintpaulias are known as a leaf petiole cutting and include a length of stalk. Select young but fully grown, healthy leaves, and cut them off cleanly near the base.

2 Trim the stalks about 1in below the leaf blade and insert so that the leaf blade sits just in contact with the cutting mixture. Insert individual cuttings in small pots, or several together in larger ones.

4 Streptocarpus can be propagated from leaf sections. Choose a healthy, mature leaf that is not very old, and with a sharp knife cut it into slices 2–3in wide.

3 Keep the cuttings moist but not wet, and the air humid. If you do not have a propagator, enclose the pot in a plastic bag, but make sure that it does not touch the leaves. Turn the bag regularly to reduce a build up of condensation. Pot up the young plantlets that form once they are growing vigorously.

5 Push the sections into the rooting mixture so that about one-third is buried. Make sure that the side originally nearest the leaf stalk forms the base. Keep the cuttings in a warm place in good light but out of direct sunlight.

LATE SPRING

LATE SPRING CAN BE DECEPTIVE. It often seems as though summer has already arrived, yet in cold areas there can be severe late frosts. Take local climate into account before planting any frost-tender plants outdoors. Even with experience it can be a gamble as an untypical season might produce surprises. Judging when frosts are no longer likely is mainly a matter of assessing risk. A good guide is to watch when summer bedding plants are put in local parks. These gardeners will have amassed generations of local knowledge of your area, which is by far the best guide.

JOBS IN BRIEF

The kitchen garden

- ☐ Plant a herb pot
- ☐ Apply manures and fertilizers where appropriate
- ☐ Sow corn outdoors in mild areas when further frost is unlikely
- ☐ Sow vegetables without protection – many kinds can be sown now, so check the packets

BELOW: *Plant a herb pot for a useful as well as a pretty display for the summer.*

- ☐ Plant potatoes
- ☐ Try a collection of mints in a growing bag
- ☐ Plant out vegetable seedlings such as cabbages and cauliflowers
- ☐ Sow seeds of crops such as cabbages, cauliflowers and sprouts in a nursery bed, where they can be grown for later transplanting
- ☐ Put straw down round strawberries or protect fruit with strawberry mats
- ☐ Sow or plant runner beans outdoors

The flower garden

- ☐ Plant and stock the pond
- ☐ Prune forsythia and *Ribes sanguineum*
- ☐ Plant container-grown shrubs
- ☐ Plant herbaceous plants
- ☐ Stake herbaceous plants
- ☐ Plant a half basket or wall pot
- ☐ Sow hardy annuals
- ☐ Plant gladioli and summer bulbs
- ☐ Mow the lawn regularly from now on
- ☐ Plant out sweet peas raised in pots
- ☐ Sow sweet peas where they are to flower
- ☐ Harden off tender bedding plants

BELOW: *Prune forsythias soon after flowering has finished.*

The greenhouse and conservatory

- ☐ Sow tender vegetables such as outdoor tomatoes and runner beans to plant out later, and cucumbers for the greenhouse
- ☐ Plant greenhouse tomatoes and cucumbers
- ☐ Feed pot-plants and seedlings regularly
- ☐ Pot on young dahlia and chrysanthemum plants if they need it
- ☐ Prick out or pot up late-sown bedding plants
- ☐ Take leaf cuttings of saintpaulias and streptocarpus

BELOW: *Plant greenhouse tomatoes provided there is sufficient warmth.*

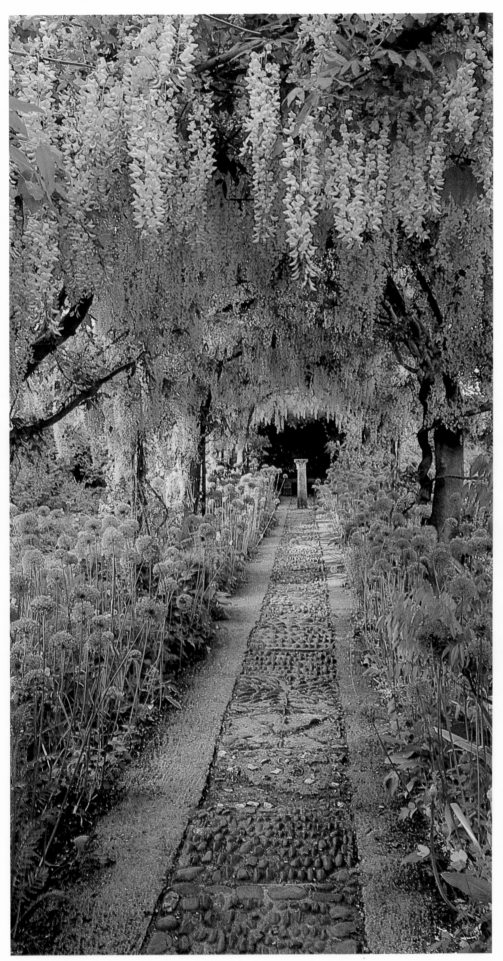

PLANTS AT THEIR BEST

Aubrieta (rock plant)
Azalea (shrub)
Bergenia (non–woody evergreen)
Calendula, autumn sown (hardy annual)
Cheiranthus (wallflower)
Choisya ternata (shrub)
Clematis montana (shrubby climber)
Crataegus (tree)
Cytisus, various (shrub)
Dicentra (herbaceous)
Fritillaria (bulb)
Genista (shrub)
Laburnum (tree)
Malus (tree)
Paeonia (herbaceous and shrub)
Phlox subulata (rock plant)
Pulsatilla vulgaris (rock plant)
Rhododendron, various (shrub)
Saxifraga, various (rock plant)
Syringa (lilac)
Tulipa, various (bulb)
Wisteria (shrubby climber)

LEFT: *Alliums beneath a laburnum arch.*

BELOW: Fritillaria meleagris.

PLANT A HERB POT

A herb pot makes an attractive feature, but it is best treated as a short-term home to be replanted annually. If you allow shrubby perennial herbs to become large and established, you will find them extremely difficult to remove when it becomes necessary. Be especially careful of planting a large shrubby plant in the top of a herb pot with a tapering neck. Once the plant has produced a mass of roots, the inward taper makes removal a frustrating task.

1 A herb pot is best filled in stages. Start by adding a good potting mixture to the height of the first planting pockets.

2 Using small plants, knock them out of their pots and push the root-balls through the holes in the planting pockets. If necessary, break off some of the root-ball so that you can get it through the hole.

3 Add more potting soil and repeat with the next row of planting holes. Unless the pot is very large, don't try to pack too many herbs into the top. A single well-grown plant often looks much better.

4 Large earthernware pots can look just as good as herb pots with planting pockets if you plant them imaginatively. If you have an old half-barrel use this instead. Place a bold shrubby herb, such as a sweet bay (*Laurus nobilis*), in the center.

5 In time the shrubby plant may take up all the planting space at the top and you will have an attractive specimen plant, but meanwhile you should be able to fit a collection of smaller herbs around the edge. Avoid mints, which may be difficult to eliminate later.

GROW MINTS

Mints are notoriously difficult to control once they make themselves at home. They send spreading and penetrating shoots beneath the surface which emerge among other plants or even the other side of a path. They are best contained in some way.

1 A growing bag is an ideal home for mints. They will be happy for a couple of seasons, and then are easily removed and replanted for a fresh start. If the mints are in large pots it may be necessary to remove some of the root-ball, but they soon recover.

2 Instead of filling the growing bag with one kind of mint, try planting a collection of perhaps four to six different kinds. This will look good and add to the flavors available for the kitchen.

OTHER HERBS TO RESTRAIN

3 If you want to plant your mint in the border (which avoids the chore of watering frequently), plant it in an old bucket or large pot. Make sure that there are drainage holes in the bottom, and fill with soil or a potting mixture and plant the mint.

4 For a visually pleasing effect, position the rim of the pot just below the level of the surrounding soil, then cover with soil to hide any signs of the pot. Lift, divide and replant annually or every second spring, to maintain vigor.

Although mint is the herb most notorious for being invasive, others can attempt a take-over of the border. Tansy (*Tanacetum vulgare*) and woodruff (*Asperula odorata* syn. *Galium odoratum*) are among the herbs that you may also want to consider planting in a plunged bucket or large pot.

SOW CORN

Corn is a reliable crop in warm areas, where it can be sown directly into the ground with confidence, but in cold regions with a short growing season, it is best to start the plants off under glass so that they have time to mature before the autumn frosts. In areas where growing conditions are less than favorable, choose a variety specially bred for a cool climate.

1 Sow only when there is no risk of frost and the soil temperature has reached 50°F. In cold areas, warm up the soil with fleece or cloches for a week or two first.

2 Sow the seeds 1in deep and 3in apart, and thin to the final recommended spacing later – typically 12in apart each way. Sow in blocks rather than single rows.

3 Cover with a fine net floating cloche or horticultural fleece. This can be left on after germination until the plants have pushed the cover up to its limit without damaging the plants.

4 In areas where outdoor sowing is unreliable, raise the plants in modules or peat pots. Plant them out when there is no danger of frost, and after careful hardening off.

PLANT OUTDOOR TOMATOES

Wait until there is little risk of frost before planting outdoor tomatoes – about the same time as you plant tender summer bedding plants. Choose varieties recommended for outdoors.

1 Plant at the spacing recommended for the variety – some grow tall and large, others remain small and compact. Always make sure they have been well hardened off.

2 In cold areas, cover plants with cloches for a few weeks, or use horticultural fleece.

3 Once the fleece or protection has been removed, stake the plants immediately. Some small varieties may not require staking.

RAISING TOMATOES IN GROWING BAGS

Tomatoes do well in growing bags, and this is a practical way to grow them on a patio as well as in a greenhouse or vegetable patch.

Staking is the main problem if you want to grow tomatoes in growing bags on a hard base. There are many ready-made designs of stake supports intended for crops like tomatoes in growing bags, and most should last for several years.

If the growing bag is positioned on soil you can simply push the stake through the bag, as shown.

PLANT RUNNER AND POLE BEANS

In mild areas runner and climbing string beans can be sown in late spring, but in cold areas wait until early summer or start the seeds off indoors. Do not plant out until there is no risk of frost.

1 Sow two seeds 2in deep by each stake or support. Thin to one plant later if both germinate. Wait until the soil temperature is at least 54°F before sowing.

2 If you raise the plants in pots, plant out once there is no reasonable risk of frost. Use a trowel and plant them just outside the stake. Train them to the stake as soon as they are tall enough.

SUPPORTING RUNNER AND POLE BEANS

Stakes and nets are the main methods of supporting runner and pole beans. If you use a net, choose a large-mesh net sold as a pea and bean net, and stretch it taut between well-secured posts. If you use stakes, the most popular methods are tepees (see right) and crossed stakes (see far right).

Ready-made supports are also available but, although usually very effective, they can be expensive.

MAKE UP A HALF-BASKET OR WALL POT

Most people love to have a traditional hanging basket, but they can be disappointing unless cared for lovingly. Even though the basket is planted with an all-around view in mind, the side nearest the wall will perform poorly in comparison with the sunny side unless you turn the basket every day or two to even up growth. A half-basket or wall pot fixed against the wall can be just as effective, and because it is planted to look good from the front only, it can be just as bold and striking as a conventional basket. Some wall pots are also decorative in their own right.

1 If the half-basket is small, you may prefer to take it down to plant it. However, drill and plug the holes, fix the hooks or screws and try it out on the wall first.

2 Add a drainage layer, such as broken pots or gravel, then partly fill with a potting mixture.

3 If using a wire half-basket, line it with moss and fill with potting mixture to the height of the first layer of plants.

4 Plant the sides, then add more moss and potting soil.

5 Plant the top of the basket with bold and spectacular plants for an eye-catching display.

6 Choose more restrained plants for a very ornamental wall pot that you want to retain as a feature in its own right.

PUTTING OUT WALL BASKETS

Half-baskets and wall pots are difficult to accommodate in the greenhouse or other sheltered and frost-free position, so it is best to wait until frost is very unlikely before planting. If you can give them a week or two in a greenhouse or cold frame, however, the plants will receive less of a check to growth and the display should be more pleasing.

RIGHT: *A genuine old manger has been used for this lavish display. Well-planted large wall pots can be just as striking.*

HARDEN OFF BEDDING PLANTS

Hardening off is a crucial stage for all plants raised indoors or in a greenhouse. If this is done properly the plants will remain sturdy and healthy, but if you move tender plants straight out into hot, dry conditions or cold biting winds outdoors after a cosseted life on the windowsill or greenhouse, losses could be high.

Plants that you buy from nurseries and garden centers should have been hardened off before you buy them.

1 Place the plants in a cold frame a week or two before planting-out time. Close the top in the evening and on cold days, otherwise ventilate freely. If frost threatens, cover the frame with insulation material or take the plants into a greenhouse or indoors again.

2 If you don't have a cold frame, cloches can be used instead. Ventilate them whenever possible so that the plants become acclimatized while still receiving protection from the worst winds and cold.

3 If you don't have frames or cloches, group the trays or pots together in a sheltered spot outside and cover them with horticultural fleece or a perforated plastic floating cloche. Take them in again if frost is forecast.

PLANT GREENHOUSE TOMATOES

Greenhouse tomatoes always used to be grown in the greenhouse border, and the soil changed periodically. This was considered risky and ring culture became fashionable. In more recent times growing bags have been in favour. Other methods are used commercially but the three practical and easy methods suitable for amateurs are described here. All three systems have merits and drawbacks, and how well you look after your tomatoes while they are growing can be as important as the system. Choose the one that appeals most or seems the easiest.

1 Always dig in as much rotted manure or garden compost as you can spare and rake in a general garden fertilizer before you plant your tomatoes. Although they can be planted earlier, most amateurs find this is a good time as the greenhouse usually has more space once the bedding plants have been moved out.

2 Most greenhouse varieties grow tall and need support. Tall stakes are a convenient method if you have just a few plants, but if you have a lot of plants the string method may be more suitable (see opposite).

3 With ring culture, the water-absorbing roots grow into a moist aggregate and the feeding roots into special bottomless pots filled with a potting mixture. Take out a trench about 6–9in deep in the greenhouse border and line it with a waterproof plastic (this minimizes soil-borne disease contamination).

4 Fill the trench with fine gravel, coarse grit or expanded clay granules. Then place the special bottomless ring culture pots on the aggregate base and fill them with a good potting mixture.

5 Plant into the ring and insert a stake or provide an alternative support. Water only into the ring at first. Once the plant is established and some roots have penetrated into the aggregate, water only the aggregate and feed through the pot.

6 Growing bags are less trouble than ring culture to set up, but you still have to feed plants regularly, and watering can be more difficult to control unless you use an automatic system. Insert a stake through the bag or use a string support.

ABOVE: *You can expect crops like this if you plant your greenhouse tomatoes now. For best results, check that the variety is recommended for greenhouse cultivation.*

SUPPORTING TOMATOES ON STRINGS

String is a simple and economical way to support your tomatoes. Fix one wire as high as practical from one end of the greenhouse to the other, aligning it above the border, and another one just above the ground. The lower wire is most conveniently fixed to a stout stake at each end of the row.

Tie lengths of string between the top and bottom wires, in line with each plant.

You don't need to tie the plant to its support, just loop the string around the growing tip so that it forms a spiral.

PLANT AND TRAIN CUCUMBERS

As with tomatoes, there are various ways to plant and train cucumbers.

Try growing cucumbers in growing bags on the greenhouse benches. Insert stakes between the growing bags and the eaves, and fix horizontal wires along the length of the roof as shown here. You can then train the growth along the roof and the cucumbers will hang down. A normal growing bag should hold about two cucumber plants. Do not over-crowd the plants.

The method shown is easy and convenient, but if you don't want the trouble of ensuring that the growing bags are kept evenly moist, you could plant the cucumbers directly into the border soil and start the horizontal wires on the sides of the greenhouse instead.

SUMMER

*Early summer is a time of intense gardening activity. Everything is
growing rapidly, in many areas tender plants can be put out, and weeds
seem to grow faster than you ever thought possible.
Mid and late summer are times for enjoying the results of your
earlier efforts. There are always jobs to be done, of course,
but you should also make time to relax.
During a dry summer water shortages can be a problem, but always
water thoroughly, as shallow, impatient watering will encourage
surface rooting and make the plants even more vulnerable.*

OPPOSITE: *Roses are part of the summer scene,
but they have even more impact when used
with imagination.*

ABOVE: *By using containers, summer color can
be brought to even the most unpromising corner
of the garden.*

EARLY SUMMER

EARLY SUMMER IS A TIME WHEN you can relax a little and enjoy all your efforts of the last few months. But there are still jobs to be done, and pests and diseases are as active as ever. Vigilance and prompt action now will often stop the trouble from spreading out of control, thus avoiding the need for more drastic control measures later.

Although there is always plenty of color at this time of year, be prepared for a few weeks when the garden is perhaps not looking at its best. Early summer is a transitional period, and there is often an interval between the spring flowering plants dying back and the peak of color offered by summer bedding plants.

JOBS IN BRIEF

The kitchen garden

- [ ] Sow corn outdoors in mild areas when further frost is extremely unlikely
- [ ] Sow vegetables – most kinds can be sown now, so check the packets. Make successional sowings of crops such as beets, carrots, lettuces and turnips
- [ ] Plant potatoes
- [ ] Plant out vegetable seedlings such as cabbages, cauliflowers, celery, corn, outdoor tomatoes and squash
- [ ] Sow seeds of crops such as cabbages, cauliflowers and sprouts in a nursery bed, where they can be grown for later transplanting
- [ ] Sow or plant runner and pole beans outdoors
- [ ] Sow string beans
- [ ] Watch out for aphids on fava beans and root flies on cabbages, carrots and onions. Prevention is better than cure

BELOW: *Thin vegetables while still small.*

The flower garden

- [ ] Dead-head border plants regularly
- [ ] Stake herbaceous plants
- [ ] Finish planting containers and baskets
- [ ] Sow hardy annuals
- [ ] Plant dahlias
- [ ] Finish planting gladioli and summer bulbs

BELOW: *Dead-head lilacs as soon as they have finished flowering.*

- [ ] Prune lilac, philadelphus, spiraea and broom
- [ ] Sow biennials such as wallflowers and forget-me-nots
- [ ] Mow the lawn except in very dry weather
- [ ] Finish hardening off and planting tender bedding plants
- [ ] Pinch out the growing tips from early-flowering chrysanthemums
- [ ] Watch out for signs of mildew and aphids on roses and spray promptly if they are found
- [ ] Apply a rose fertilizer once the main flush of flowering is over

The greenhouse and conservatory

- [ ] Feed pot-plants regularly
- [ ] Take leaf cuttings of saintpaulias and streptocarpus
- [ ] Start to feed tomatoes when the first truss of fruit has set
- [ ] Try biological pest control for greenhouse pests
- [ ] Pot up and pot on seedling pot-plants as it becomes necessary

BELOW: *Check pot-plants regularly to make sure they are receiving enough water.*

BELOW: *Biological pest controls can be very successful if used properly.*

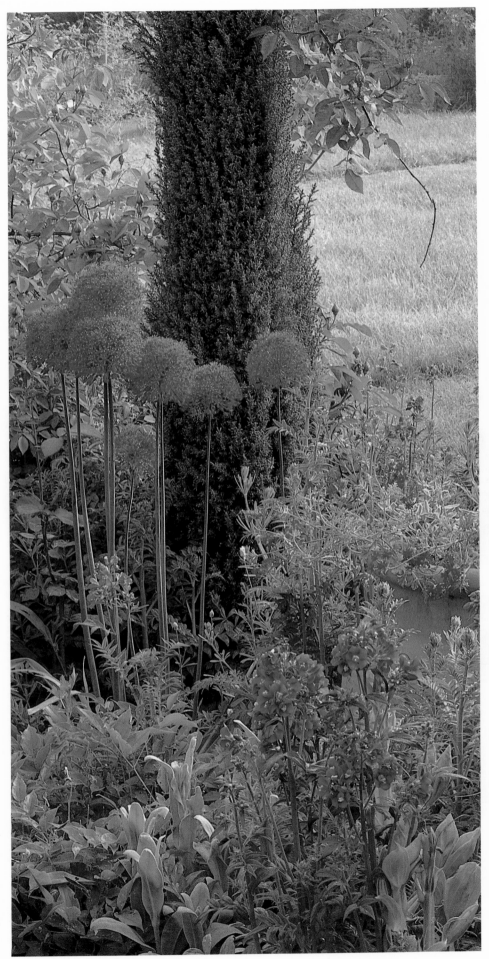

PLANTS AT THEIR BEST

Alchemilla mollis (herbaceous)
Allium (bulb)
Buddleia globosa (shrub)
Calendula (hardy annual)
Cistus (shrub)
Dianthus (carnations and pinks)
Digitalis (biennial)
Geranium (herbaceous)
Godetia (hardy annual)
Iris germanica hybrids (border irises)
Laburnum (tree)
Lupinus (herbaceous)
Paeonia (herbaceous)
Papaver orientale (herbaceous)
Philadelphus (shrub)
Rosa (most types of rose)
Weigela (shrub)

LEFT: *Early summer is full of promise.*

BELOW: Philadelphus *x* lemoinei.

BOTTOM: Dianthus *'Caesar's Bloody Pink.'*

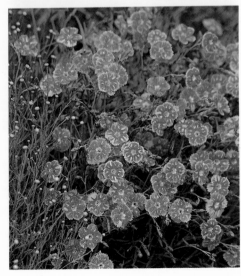

PROTECT AND EARTH UP POTATOES

Potatoes are earthed up to protect the tubers near the surface from light. If they are exposed, their skins will turn green and the tubers will be completely inedible.

1 Potatoes will usually recover from slight frost damage, but if you know that a frost is forecast once the shoots are through the ground try covering the plants with newspaper or horticultural fleece. Peg into position, then remove the next morning or when the frost has gone.

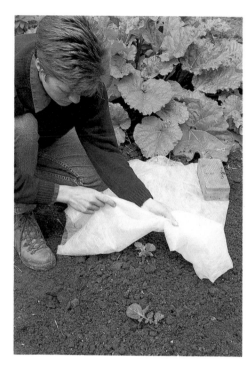

2 Start earthing up the potatoes when the shoots are about 6in high. Use a draw hoe to pull up the soil either side of the row.

3 Continue to earth up in stages, as the potatoes grow, until the soil creates a mound about 6in high.

THIN SEEDLINGS

Thinning is a tedious but essential task. The final spacing between plants will determine both the size of the individual vegetables and the total yield. Exact spacing will often depend on whether you are more interested in the total crop or large, well-shaped individual specimens.

1 Follow the spacing advice given on the seed packet when sowing. It should also recommend the ideal final spacing between plants after thinning.

2 Thin in stages, pulling up surplus plants between finger and thumb. The first thinning should leave the plants twice as close as their final spacing, to allow for losses after thinning.

3 Before the plants begin to compete with each other, thin once more to the final spacing.

SOWING MINI-CAULIFLOWERS

Mini-cauliflowers are summer varieties sown in spring or early summer but grown at much closer spacing than normal. Sow several seeds every 6in where they are to grow, and thin these to one seedling if more than one germinates. The heads are much smaller than normal, but total yield can still be good.

MULTIPLE SOWING

Some gardeners grow certain vegetables – such as carrots, beets, onions and leeks, in small clusters. Four to six seeds are usually sown in each cell of modular trays (see top), and planted out without any attempt to separate them. These are not normally thinned. The vegetables are usually smaller and less well shaped than those sown in rows and thinned normally, but the overall weight of crop may be good if the spacing recommended for this type of cultivation is followed (see above).

TRANSPLANTING SEEDLINGS

Do not attempt to transplant spare thinnings of root crops such as carrots and turnips, but other crops – like lettuces and cabbages, for example – can transplant satisfactorily.

The secret of success is to water the row thoroughly an hour before you thin or transplant (check to make sure that moisture has penetrated to root level), and to lift the spare seedlings with as much soil as possible around the roots. Always water well until plants recover, and shade from direct sun for a few days.

LEFT: *The total yield can sometimes be higher from close spacing, even though individual specimens are smaller.*

SUMMER TROUGHS AND WINDOWBOXES

Frost-tender bedding plants can now be planted in all but the coldest areas, but be guided by local conditions. Tubs and troughs packed with summer bedding plants are a sure-fire way to bring pockets of cheerful color to parts of the garden that would not otherwise be so colorful. Make the most of windowboxes, too, which will brighten the exterior of any home.

1 Windowboxes and troughs can be planted in the same way – but for a windowbox include more trailers than you would for a trough. Always make sure that there are drainage holes, and add a drainage layer such as broken pots or gravel.

2 Half fill the box or trough with a good potting mix – a loam-based one can be used for troughs, but if the windowbox is to be fixed on brackets choose a lightweight mixture based on peat or a peat substitute.

3 Most people prefer a mixed planting, with some trailers and both flowering and foliage plants. Try arranging the plants before actually planting to help visualize how they will look.

SINGLE-SUBJECT PLANTING

Most people plant mixed groups, but sometimes a single-subject planting can look especially striking. Impatiens and begonia are popular plants suitable for this treatment, but be prepared to experiment with others.

Because single-subject plants have an even height, it is important to choose a container that is in proportion to the plants. For example, compact begonias look lost in a deep trough, but are in keeping with a shallow windowbox.

4 When the positions look right, insert the plants, firming the potting mix around each root-ball. Plant more closely than in beds or borders, so avoid using plants that will overpower their neighbours.

5 Water thoroughly after planting, and make sure that the soil mix never dries out. In warm weather this means watering daily, sometimes more than once.

PLANT TUBS AND PATIO POTS

Although all the plants suitable for windowboxes and troughs can be used in tubs and large patio pots, the greater depth of potting soil offers scope for larger and often bolder plants, and the circular shape generally demands an eye-catching plant as a centerpiece. Trailers will enhance a plain container, but if you have a very ornate or decorative pot, it may be best to plant trailers with restraint so that the pot itself remains a feature in its own right.

1 Filled tubs and pots can be very heavy to move, so plant them where they are to be displayed. Cover the drainage holes with a layer of broken pots, gravel or chipped bark.

2 A loam-based potting mixture is best for most plants, but if the pot is to be used where weight is a consideration, such as on a balcony, use a peat-based mixture.

3 Choose a tall or bold plant for the center, such as *Cordyline australis* or a fuchsia, or one with large flowers such as the osteospermum which has been used here.

4 Fill in around the base with some bushier but lower-growing plants. Choose bright flowers if the centerpiece is a foliage plant, but place the emphasis on foliage effect if the focal-point is a flowering plant.

5 Cover the surface with a decorative mulch such as chipped bark or cocoa shells if much of the surface is visible (this is worth doing anyway to conserve moisture). Water thoroughly.

ABOVE: *Even a simple poppy can make an impact if the container itself is interesting.*

SOW BIENNIALS AND HARDY PERENNIALS

Biennials such as wallflowers and forget-me-nots are very easy to raise from seed, and because they can be sown outdoors they need very little attention. Border perennials such as lupines and aquilegias are also easily raised from seed sown now, and some of them may even flower next summer. Others may take another year or so to establish before flowering.

1 Prepare the ground thoroughly, and eliminate as many weeds as possible. Competition from weeds is often the greatest enemy the seedlings face. Break the soil down into a fine, crumbly structure once it has been cleared of weeds.

2 Open up drills with the corner of a hoe or rake to the recommended depth (this varies with the seed, so check the packet). The drills can be quite close together, because the seedlings will be transplanted as soon as they are large enough.

3 Run water into the drill before sowing if the soil is very dry. Space the seeds thinly, and as evenly as you can. This makes thinning and later transplanting much easier.

4 Cover the seeds by shuffling the soil back with your feet or carefully ease the soil back with the back of a rake. Remember to add a label.

5 Thin the seedlings as soon as they are large enough to handle easily so that they do not become overcrowded.

ABOVE: *Wallflowers are one of the most popular biennials, and really easy to grow from seeds sown now.*

PRUNE SHRUBS

Many shrubs thrive without routine annual pruning, but some that flower in spring or early summer benefit from pruning soon after they have finished flowering. These include *Cytisus* (brooms), *Syringas* (lilacs), philadelphus, and spring-flowering spiraeas.

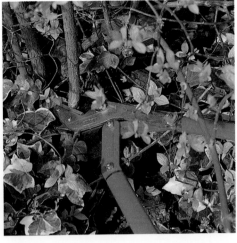

1 Philadelphus (illustrated) and spring-flowering spiraeas such as *Spiraea × arguta* and *S. thunbergii* become too dense and overcrowded if they are not pruned. Annual pruning keeps them compact and flowering well, and the best time to do this is immediately after flowering.

2 Reduce the shoots by one-third, cutting out the oldest ones. Cut back the old stems to where a new shoot is growing lower down, or to just above the ground if the shoot is very old and the bush very congested.

RENOVATING AN OLD LILAC

Very old *Syringa vulgaris* varieties often become tall and leggy, with the flowers very high up. You may be able to rejuvenate a neglected plant by sawing it down to a height of 12in–3ft. This sounds drastic, and the lilac will not flower for a year or two, but it should shoot from the old wood and produce an attractive compact plant again.

3 Brooms and genistas tend to become woody at the base with age, with the flowers too high up the plants to look attractive. Prune them as soon as the flowers die and the seed pods are beginning to form.

4 Cut back each shoot to about half way along the new green growth. Do not count dark, old wood, and do not cut back into this as new shoots will be reluctant to grow. You will not be able to make an old neglected plant bush from the base – start regular pruning from an early stage.

5 Lilacs benefit from careful dead-heading. As soon as the flowering is over, cut the dead blooms back to the first pair of leaves below the flower head (no further, otherwise you might remove buds from which new flowering shoots will be produced).

FEEDING AND WATERING IN THE GREENHOUSE

Watering is a year-round chore in the greenhouse, but the summer months are even more demanding. Consider an automatic or semi-automatic watering system to make lighter work of the job. Most pot-plants respond readily to regular feeding during the growing season, but underfeeding is not easy to detect until the plants have been starved for some time.

1 Plants should be watered before they show obvious signs of distress such as wilting. With bushy plants it is not possible to judge by the visual appearance of the potting mixture either, and touch is often the only practical guide. However, this is both time-consuming and only reasonably accurate.

2 Moisture indicators for individual pots can be helpful for a beginner, or if there are just a few plants, but they are not a practical solution if you have a whole greenhouse or conservatory full of plants.

3 Capillary matting is an ideal way to water most pot-plants in summer. You can use a ready-made system fed by water pipes, or improvise with a system like the one illustrated. This uses a length of gutter for the water supply. You can keep it topped up by hand, with special water bags or from a cistern.

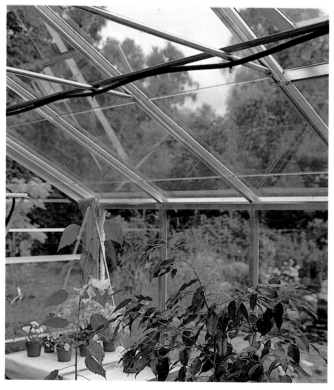

4 If watering by hand, use the can without a rose unless you are watering seedlings. This will enable you to direct water more easily to the roots rather than sprinkling the leaves. Use a finger over the end of the spout to control the flow, or stick a rag in the end to break the force.

5 An overhead spray system operated automatically or when you turn on the tap is useful for a large greenhouse, either for plants on benches or those planted in the border. Water is not so carefully directed to where it is needed, so it is not ideal for pot-plants, but the spray helps to create a humid atmosphere.

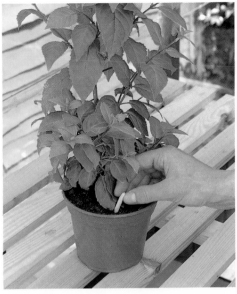

6 Use a liquid fertilizer applied with the water if you can remember to do it regularly. There are both soluble powders and liquids that can be diluted to the appropriate strength.

7 Fertilizer sticks and tablets that you push into the potting soil are a convenient way to administer fertilizer if you don't want to apply liquid feeds regularly. Most of these release their nutrients over a period of several months.

BIOLOGICAL CONTROLS

The greenhouse or conservatory is an ideal place to practice biological control methods – the predators will thrive in the protected environment, and should multiply rapidly until control is achieved.

1 Various forms of biological controls are available for a number of greenhouse pests. *Encarsia formosa* is a tiny wasp that parasitizes whitefly larvae and eventually kills them. There are other predatory wasps and mites that will attack red spider, soft scale insects, and thrips.

2 If weevil grubs destroy your plants by eating the roots, try controlling them in future with a parasitic eelworm. A suspension of the eelworms is simply watered over the potting soil in each pot.

ALTERNATIVE FERTILIZERS

Use a general-purpose fertilizer if you want to avoid using different foods for different plants: this is better than not feeding at all.

Some fertilizers are described as being specially formulated for either foliage plants or flowering plants, however, and these will suit the majority of plants within each category. But if you have to feed both flowering and foliage plants with the one fertilizer, these are unlikely to do any harm.

Some enthusiasts prefer to use special feeds for certain types of plant, such as saintpaulias and cacti, but these will also respond to fertilizers used for other pot-plants.

Fertilizers formulated for strong feeders such as tomatoes and chrysanthemums should only be used on other plants with care – they may be too strong.

WORKING WITH BIOLOGICAL CONTROLS

Biological controls usually work best when the weather is warm, and some are unsuitable for use outdoors. Use pesticides with care, as they can wipe out your predators as well as the harmful insects and you will destroy the balance between the two.

With biological controls you will always have some pests – they are essential for the predator to be able to continue to breed – but only at a low population level.

AIR LAYER LEGGY PLANTS

Some hardy plants such as magnolias and rhododendrons can be air layered outside, but the technique is most often used for indoor and greenhouse plants that have become tall and bare at the base. Instead of an unattractive 'leggy' plant you can start off again with a reasonably sized specimen that looks good from top to pot. *Ficus elastica* is commonly treated this way, but other plants, such as dracaenas, are worth trying.

Plants can be air layered at almost any time, but early summer is ideal because they are growing vigorously in the increasing light and warmth.

1 Layer the plant above the bare area, just below the leaves. If you are using the technique on a multi-stemmed plant just to increase stock, remove a few leaves from the point where you want to make the layer.

2 Carefully make an upward slit about 1in long, below an old leaf joint. Do not cut more than half-way through the stem, otherwise the shoot may break.

3 Make a sleeve out of plastic sheet. It does not have to form a tube as you can wrap it round the stem then make a seal. Fix the bottom of the sleeve a short distance below the cut, using a twist-tie or adhesive tape.

4 Brush a small amount of rooting hormone (powder or gel) into the wound, to speed rooting. Then pack a little sphagnum moss into the wound to keep it open.

5 Pack plenty of damp sphagnum moss around the stem, to enclose the wound, then cover with the sheet of plastic and secure at the top with another twist-tie or tape. Make sure that the moss is kept moist, and carefully check for roots after a month or so. When well rooted, sever from the parent and pot up.

DIVIDE CONGESTED POT-PLANTS

Once a plant has filled its pot and if it is not practical to move it to a larger one, division may revive it and will also give you a number of extra plants. Not all plants respond to division. Those with a fibrous root system, like calatheas and most ferns, are more likely to divide successfully.

A few flowering plants bloom better if kept slightly pot-bound. Check if a particular plant responds well to division in an encyclopedia.

House and greenhouse plants can be divided throughout the year, but late spring and early summer are particularly good times.

1 Water the plant at least half an hour before you divide it. If the plant will not come out of the pot easily, try inverting the pot while you support the plant and tap its rim on a hard surface.

2 Remove any broken pots used to cover the old drainage hole in a clay pot, and pull away a little potting soil to expose some of the roots and make division easier.

3 Most plants can be pulled apart by hand, but if the root-ball is difficult to break open this way use a hand fork.

4 Break the clump into smaller pieces. If you want many plants, divide into quite small pieces, but if you need only one or two, and prefer to start again with larger plants, two or three pieces may be appropriate. It may be necessary to trim off a few of the largest roots to fit the plant in its new pot.

5 Replant sections as soon as possible, trickling potting soil around the roots. If possible, use the same kind of potting material as the plant was in before, and firm it well around the roots. Water and keep out of direct sunlight for a few days.

MID SUMMER

MID SUMMER IS MAINLY A TIME to enjoy your garden, rather than do a lot of physical work in it. Most things are already sown or planted, and the emphasis is on weeding and watering. Regular dead-heading will keep the garden looking tidy and benefit the plants too.

JOBS IN BRIEF

The kitchen garden

- ☐ Hoe regularly to keep down weeds
- ☐ Sow more vegetables – including spinach, parsley, and (in cold areas) spring cabbage. Make successional sowings of crops such as beets, carrots, lettuces and turnips
- ☐ Continue to thin vegetables sown earlier, before they grow large enough to compete with each other
- ☐ Plant out late cauliflowers, winter cabbages, and leeks
- ☐ Sow more string beans
- ☐ Give plants that need a boost a dressing dose of quick-acting fertilizer, but if using a powder or granules be sure to water in thoroughly
- ☐ Pinch out the growing tips of runner beans when they reach the top of their support
- ☐ Lift shallots if they have finished growing, and leave them on the surface for a few days to dry off
- ☐ Harvest herbs regularly. Don't let the leaves become too old
- ☐ Thin apples
- ☐ Summer prune cordon and espalier apples
- ☐ Tidy up summer-flowering strawberries that have finished fruiting. Cut off old leaves and unwanted runners, remove straw, and control weeds
- ☐ Remain vigilant for early signs of pests and diseases. Caterpillars can devastate a cabbage crop if undetected
- ☐ Water vulnerable crops before they show signs of stress

The flower garden

- ☐ Dead-head border plants regularly
- ☐ Hoe beds and borders regularly to keep down weeds
- ☐ Divide and replant border irises
- ☐ Take semi-ripe cuttings
- ☐ Clip beech, holly, hornbeam and yew hedges towards the end of the period
- ☐ Layer shrubs and carnations
- ☐ Plant colchicums, to flower in the autumn, when they are available
- ☐ Transplant biennials and perennial seedlings to a nursery bed
- ☐ Order bulb catalogues and bulbs for autumn delivery
- ☐ Disbud early-flowering chrysanthemums
- ☐ Mow the lawn except in very dry weather
- ☐ Watch out for signs of mildew and aphids on roses and spray promptly if they are found

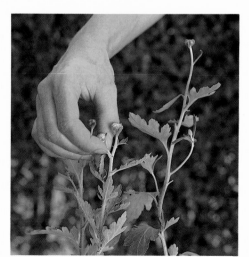

BELOW: *Disbud chrysanthemums if you want larger flowers later.*

The greenhouse and conservatory

- ☐ Feed pot-plants regularly
- ☐ Take leaf and semi-ripe cuttings
- ☐ Feed tomatoes and chrysanthemums regularly
- ☐ Remove sideshoots and yellowing leaves from tomatoes regularly
- ☐ Keep a vigilant watch for pests and diseases. Spray promptly or try a biological control for greenhouse pests
- ☐ Pot up and pot on seedling pot-plants as it becomes necessary

BELOW: *Do not forget to feed. Slow-release sticks like this make it a less frequent chore.*

BELOW: *Regularly remove sideshoots from cordon tomatoes (leave them on bush types).*

ABOVE: *Lilies like this 'Connecticut King' make stunning border plants.*

BELOW: *Mid summer sees the garden at its most beautiful.*

PLANTS AT THEIR BEST

Alchemilla mollis (herbaceous)
Althaea (herbaceous)
Astilbe (herbaceous)
Cistus (shrub)
Clematis (shrubby climber)
Dianthus (carnations and pinks)
Digitalis (biennial)
Geranium (herbaceous)
Hardy annuals (many)
Helianthemum (shrub)
Hydrangea (shrub)
Hypericum (shrub)
Kniphofia (herbaceous)
Lavandula (shrub)
Lilium (bulb)
Potentilla (shrub)
Rosa (most types of rose)
Summer bedding plants
Verbascum (herbaceous)

CONTROL WEEDS

It is never possible to eliminate weeds entirely, but you can control them. Even weeds that are difficult to eradicate can be conquered if you persist, and annual weeds will diminish in numbers if you continue to kill off the seedlings before they can flower and shed more seed.

Once the weed population has been reduced, mulching and prompt action to remove the seedlings that do appear will keep the garden almost weed-free. Be prepared for the battle to be won over a couple of seasons rather than in a few weeks if the garden has been neglected.

1 Deep-rooted perennial weeds that have long, penetrating roots are best forked up. Loosen the roots with a fork, and hold the stem close to its base as you pull up the whole plant. If you don't get all the root out, new pieces may grow.

2 Hoeing is one of the best forms of weed control, but it needs to be done regularly. Slice the weeds off just beneath the soil, preferably when the soil is dry. Keep beds and borders hoed, as well as the vegetable garden.

3 Contact chemical weedkillers are useful if you need to clear an area of ground quickly and easily. Some – which normally only kill the top growth, so are better for annuals than problem perennial weeds – leave the area safe to replant after a day.

4 Some weedkillers kill the whole plant, including the roots. Large areas of ground can be sprayed, but you can paint some formulations onto the leaves to kill the weed without harming neighboring plants.

5 Mulches are very effective at controlling weeds. In the vegetable and fruit garden various forms of plastic sheeting are a cost-effective method.

6 Where appearance matters, use an organic material such as chipped bark, garden compost or cocoa shells. If the ground is cleared of weeds first, a mulch at least 2in thick will suppress most weeds.

SUMMER PRUNE CORDON AND ESPALIER APPLES

Shaped and trained apple trees are normally pruned twice a year – once in summer and again in winter. Summer pruning controls the amount of growth produced each year and maintains the basic shape, winter pruning consists of thinning overcrowded fruiting spurs on old plants. In late spring the new growth at the ends of the main shoots is cut back to its point of origin, but summer pruning is the most crucial in terms of maintaining the trained shape.

ESPALIER

1 Shorten new leafy shoots that have grown directly from the main branches back to three leaves above the basal cluster of leaves. This should only be done once the shoots have dark green leaves and the bark has started to turn brown and is woody at the base. In cold areas it may be early autumn before the shoots are mature enough.

2 If the shoot is growing from a stub left by previous pruning – and not directly from one of the main stems – cut back to just one leaf above the basal cluster of leaves.

CORDON

1 A cordon is pruned in exactly the same way as an espalier, although, of course, the basic shape of the plant is different. Just cut back shoots growing directly from the main branch to three leaves above the basal cluster of leaves.

2 Cut back shoots growing from stubs left by earlier pruning to one leaf above the basal cluster.

TAKE SEMI-RIPE CUTTINGS

Semi-ripe cuttings – also known as semi-mature cuttings – can be used to propagate a wide range of shrubs, both hardy and tender. If you take them in mid or late summer most will root quickly, and in the case of hardy plants you don't even need a propagator.

1 Choose shoots that are almost fully grown except for the soft tip. The base of the cutting should be hardening, even though the tip may still be soft. Most cuttings are best made 2–4in long.

2 Strip the lower leaves from each plant to leave a short length of clear stem to insert into the soil.

3 It is well worth using a rooting hormone. Dip the cut end into the powder, liquid or gel, but if using a powder dip the ends into water first so that the powder adheres.

4 Cuttings taken from hardy plants will root outside at this time of year, though they will perform better in a cold frame or propagator.

5 Firm the cuttings to ensure there are no large pockets of air, which might cause the new roots to dry out.

6 Remember to insert a label. This is especially important if you are rooting a number of different kinds of shrubs.

SOME SHRUBS TO PROPAGATE FROM SEMI-RIPE CUTTINGS

Buddleia	*Fuchsia*
Camellia	*Griselinia*
Ceanothus	*Hebe*
Choisya	*Hydrangea*
Cistus	*Philadelphus*
Cotoneaster	*Potentilla*
(illustrated)	*Pyracantha*
Escallonia	*Rosemary*
Forsythia	*Weigela*

7 Water thoroughly. It is worth adding a fungicide to the water initially, to reduce the chance of the cuttings rotting. Make sure that the soil does not dry out at any time.

LAYER SHRUBS

Layering is usually used for shrubby plants that have low branches easily pegged to the ground, but a few border plants can also be layered – carnations and pinks are often raised this way. In comparison with cuttings, layers usually produce fewer but bigger plants.

1 Find a low-growing shoot that can easily be pegged down to the ground. Trim off the leaves just from the area that will be in contact with the soil.

2 Bend the stem down until it touches the ground. Make a hole 4in deep, sloping toward the parent plant but with the other side vertical.

3 Twist or slit the stem slightly to injure it. Peg it into the hole with a piece of bent wire or a peg, using the vertical back of the excavation to force the shoot upright.

4 Return the soil and firm it well. If you keep the ground moist, roots should form and within 12–18 months you may be able to sever the new plant from its parent.

DIVIDE FLAG IRISES

Divide flag irises – hybrids derived from *Iris germanica* – after flowering and if the rhizomes have become very congested.

1 Lift the clump with a fork, and cut away and discard the oldest parts. Use only the current season's growth for replanting.

2 Trim the leaves to stumps about 2–3in long. Replant the pieces of rhizome on a slight ridge of soil, covering the roots with soil but leaving the tops exposed.

LAYERING CARNATIONS

Border carnations and pinks are layered in a similar way to shrubs, but root much more quickly. Select a few well-spaced, non-flowering shoots and remove all but the top four or five leaves on them. Make a small slit in each one with a sharp knife below the lowest pair of leaves, and peg the shoot – slit down – into good soil. Keep moist.

SUMMER CARE FOR GREENHOUSE TOMATOES

The varieties of tomato usually grown in the greenhouse need regular attention, like the removal of sideshoots, feeding, and tying in.

Keep a watch too for early signs of pests and diseases that could otherwise reduce the quantity or quality of the crop.

1 If the plants are supported by strings, simply loop the string around the top of the shoot whenever necessary. It will form a spiral support that holds the stem upright.

2 To secure the plant to a stake, wrap the string twice around the stake and then loop it loosely around the stem before tying the knot.

3 Snap off sideshoots while they are still small. They will snap off cleanly if you pull them sideways. Do not remove sideshoots if you have a low-growing bush variety.

4 If fruits are failing to form, poor pollination may be the problem. Shake the plants each day, or spray the flowers with water, to spread the pollen.

5 The lowest leaves often turn yellow as they age. Remove these, as they will not contribute to feeding the plant, and letting more light reach the fruits can help to ripen them.

6 'Stop' your plants, by removing the growing tip, when they have formed as many trusses of fruit as are likely to ripen. In an unheated greenhouse this may be as few as four in cold areas; six or seven in warmer regions.

7 Tomatoes respond well to feeding. Some tomato feeds are high in nitrogen for early growth, but now that the fruit is developing, a high-potash tomato fertilizer is best.

OTHER GREENHOUSE CROPS

Greenhouse crops like eggplants, cucumbers and melons also need attention at this time of year if you want to ensure a good, healthy crop.

CARING FOR MELONS

Train the sideshoot of melons to horizontal wires, and pinch back the sideshoots to two leaves beyond each fruit that develops. Melons may require pollinating, in which case transfer the pollen from the male to female flowers with a small paintbrush. It may also be necessary to support developing fruits with nets, as shown.

1 Eggplants make bushier plants if the growing tip is pinched out when the plant is about 12in high. Allow only one fruit to develop on each shoot. Pinch out the growing tips of these shoots three leaves beyond the developing fruit. Never let the plants dry out, and feed regularly. Regular misting to provide high humidity is beneficial.

2 Many modern cucumbers produce only female flowers, but there are some varieties you might grow in a greenhouse that produce both male and female blooms (the female flowers have a small embryo fruit behind the petals). Pinch out male flowers before they have a chance to pollinate the female ones, as this can make the cucumbers less palatable.

DAMPING DOWN

Splashing or spraying water over the greenhouse path (traditionally known as damping down) helps to create a humid atmosphere. This is especially beneficial for crops such as eggplants and cucumbers, but most plants appreciate a moist atmosphere on a hot day – including the majority of pot-plants. Do it frequently on very hot days, to create the kind of hot and humid atmosphere that most tropical plants prefer.

LATE SUMMER

LATE SUMMER IS USUALLY A TIME of hot, dry weather, when there is a natural lull in the garden, and the efforts of spring and early summer sowing and planting will have paid dividends. The chores of early autumn can wait until holidays are over and cooler weather begins to return. Most of this month's work in the garden involves watering and routine maintenance tasks like mowing and hoeing, and clipping hedges.

JOBS IN BRIEF

The kitchen garden

- ☐ Hoe regularly to keep down weeds
- ☐ Lift onions and shallots as they become ready
- ☐ Continue to thin vegetables sown earlier
- ☐ Give plants that need a boost a dose of a quick-acting fertilizer
- ☐ Sow cabbages for spring use
- ☐ Pinch out the growing tips of runner beans when they reach the top of their support
- ☐ Pay regular attention to outdoor tomatoes
- ☐ Continue to harvest herbs regularly
- ☐ Summer prune cordon and espalier apples if not already done so and shoots are mature enough
- ☐ Tidy up summer-flowering strawberries. Cut off old leaves and unwanted runners, remove straw, and control weeds
- ☐ Protect fruit against birds if they are troublesome. A fruit cage is ideal

BELOW: *Harvest herbs for a fresh supply of culinary seasonings.*

The flower garden

- ☐ Dead-head plants in borders and containers regularly
- ☐ Feed plants in containers to keep the blooms coming
- ☐ Hoe beds and borders regularly to keep down weeds
- ☐ Take semi-ripe cuttings
- ☐ Clip beech, holly, hornbeam and yew hedges, and most evergreen hedges, if not already done so
- ☐ Plant colchicums, to flower in the autumn
- ☐ Order bulb catalogues and bulbs for autumn delivery
- ☐ Start planting spring-flowering bulbs
- ☐ Take fuchsia and pelargonium cuttings
- ☐ Start sowing hardy annuals to overwinter (only in mild areas or if you can provide winter protection)
- ☐ Prune rambler roses
- ☐ Layer border carnations
- ☐ Mow the lawn except in very dry weather
- ☐ Water the lawn in dry spells, but a few good soaks will be better than many sprinklings that do not penetrate deeply
- ☐ Watch out for pests and diseases on roses and other vulnerable plants
- ☐ Feed and disbud dahlias and chrysanthemums as necessary
- ☐ Transplant primrose seedlings into their flowering positions in beds and borders
- ☐ Keep paths and drives weed-free by hand or with a weedkiller

The greenhouse and conservatory

- ☐ Sow spring-flowering plants such as cyclamen, schizanthus and exacums
- ☐ Continue to feed pot-plants regularly
- ☐ Take leaf and semi-ripe cuttings
- ☐ Continue to feed tomatoes and to deal with routine tasks
- ☐ Keep a vigilant watch for pests and diseases
- ☐ Pot up and pot on seedling pot-plants as it becomes necessary
- ☐ Plant hyacinths for early flowering under glass

BELOW: *Plant prepared hyacinths for early flowering as soon as they are available.*

- ☐ Check cinerarias for leaf miners (white 'tunnels' in the leaves). Remove affected leaves or control with a systemic insecticide

PLANTS AT THEIR BEST

Dahlia (bulb)
Erigeron (herbaceous)
Fuchsia (shrub)
Helenium (herbaceous)
Hibiscus syriacus (shrub)
Hydrangea (shrub)
Hypericum (shrub)
Lavatera (shrub)
Lilium (bulb)
Perovskia atriplicifolia (shrub)
Romneya (shrub)
Solidago (herbaceous)
Summer bedding plants
Verbascum (herbaceous)

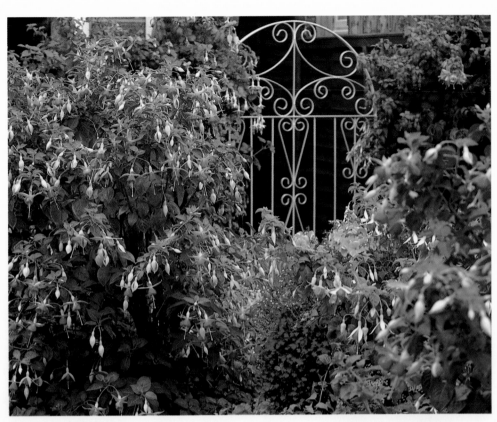

RIGHT: *Fuchsias flower throughout the summer and will continue into autumn.*

BELOW: Perovskia atriplicifolia *'Blue Spire' is one of the best blue flowers for late summer, and is undemanding to grow.*

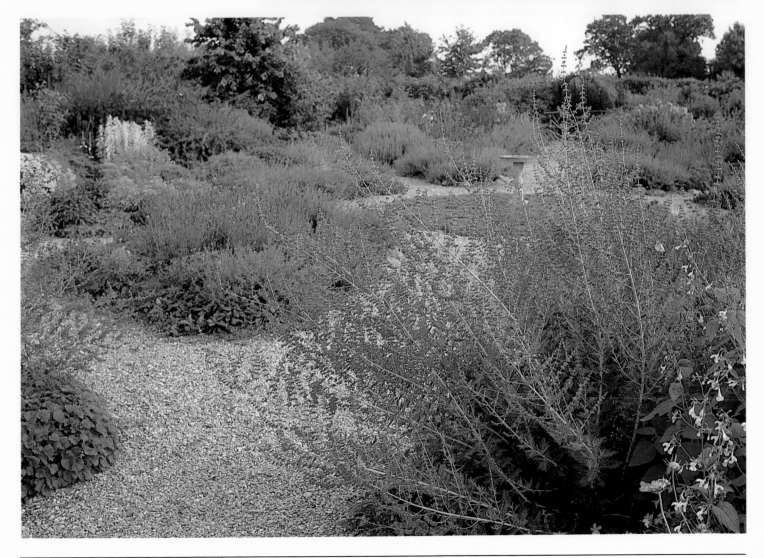

SUMMER CARE FOR OUTDOOR TOMATOES

Outdoor tomatoes demand less attention than greenhouse varieties, especially if you grow the kinds where you leave on the sideshoots. Feeding and watering is a necessary routine if you want a good crop of quality fruits. Regular watering not only ensures a heavy crop but also reduces the risk of fruit splitting through uneven watering. This sometimes happens if dry weather produces hard skins which then can't cope with a sudden spurt of growth following a wet period. Add a liquid fertilizer to the water, at the rate and frequency recommended by the manufacturer. How well your tomatoes bear outdoors depends on a combination of variety, care and climate. In cold areas, outdoor tomatoes can be a disappointing crop, in warm areas you will almost certainly have more fruit than you can cope with.

1 If growing a cordon variety (one that you grow as a single main stem, supported by a stake), keep removing sideshoots as they develop.

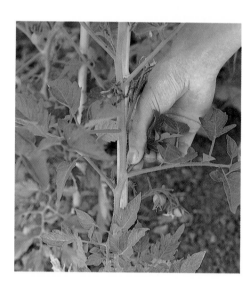

2 Regular tying to the support is even more important out-doors than in the greenhouse, as strong winds can break an untied stem and shorten the productive life of the plant.

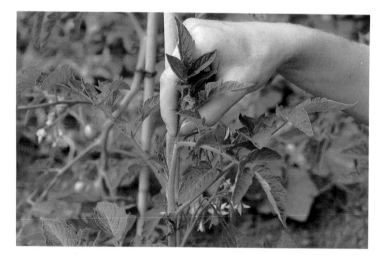

3 As soon as the plant has set the number of trusses (sprays) of fruit likely to be ripened in your area, pinch out the top of the plant. In many areas you can only reasonably expect to ripen four trusses, but in warm areas it may be more.

4 Many bush varieties have small but prolific fruits. As it is not practical to support all the sideshoots with stakes, some branches bend and come into contact with the soil. Place straw beneath these to keep the fruits off the soil. It will keep them cleaner and reduce the risk of them rotting.

LIFT SHALLOTS

Shallots usually stop growing before onions and, if planted early, can be lifted in mid summer.

But if you planted late it may be late summer before they are ready to ripen and harvest.

1 Loosen the clumps with a fork, but leave them exposed on the surface for a few days. This will give the base of the bulb a chance to dry off before being stored.

2 If the weather is damp, leave the bulbs on trays in a light, warm place so that they are not damp when stored. Or leave them on mesh trays out-doors until dry (see onions, step 3).

RIPEN AND HARVEST ONIONS

Harvest onions when the foliage is straw colored and brittle dry. They will store better if,

when lifted, they are exposed to the sun to ripen and dry first.

1 Ripening can be hastened once the plants are nearing their maximum size by bending over their tops. Bend them so that the bulbs are exposed to as much sun as possible.

2 As soon as the foliage has turned a straw color and is brittle, lift them with a fork and leave them on the surface for a few days to dry off. Lay with their roots facing the sun.

3 Finish off the hardening and ripening process by laying the bulbs on netting or wire mesh supported above the ground so that air can circulate freely.

4 If the weather is very damp, cover the bulbs with cloches until you can store them.

TAKE FUCHSIA CUTTINGS

Fuchsias are really easy to root, and by taking cuttings now you will have young plants that can be overwintered in a light position in a cool but frost-free room or in a greenhouse. These will make good plants for next summer, or you can use them to provide more cuttings next spring.

1 Softwood cuttings can be taken for as long as new growth is being produced, but at this time of year semi-ripe (semi-mature) cuttings root easily and are simple to take. Pull off sideshoots about 4in long, with a 'heel' of old main stem attached.

2 Trim off the lowest leaves and trim the end of the heel to make a clean cut. If you have taken cuttings without a heel, trim the stem straight across beneath a leaf-joint.

3 Although cuttings will usually root without aid, a hormone rooting powder should speed the process. Insert several cuttings around the edge of a 3–4in pot filled with a rooting mixture.

4 Label the cuttings, water and place them in a cold frame, greenhouse or on a light windowsill. Keep the soil mix damp, and pot up individually when well rooted. Protect from frost.

TAKE PELARGONIUM CUTTINGS

Pelargoniums (popularly known as bedding geraniums) can be overwintered in a frost-free place to provide cuttings next spring. Many experts prefer to take cuttings now, however, and to overwinter the young plants in a light, frost-free place.

RIGHT: *Pelargoniums, or bedding geraniums, are one of the most popular of summer plants.*

1 Take cuttings from non-flowering shoots (if you have to use flowering shoots, cut off the blooms). A good guide to length is to cut the shoot off just above the third joint below the growing tip.

2 Remove the lowest pair of leaves with a sharp knife, and remove any flowers or buds. Trim straight across the base of each cutting, just below the lowest leaf joint. You can dip the ends in a rooting hormone, but they usually root readily without.

3 Insert about five cuttings around the edge of a 5in pot containing a rooting mixture and firm gently. Keep the pot in a light, warm position but out of direct sunlight. Be careful not to overwater, otherwise the cuttings will rot. Pot up individually when rooted.

DAHLIA AND CHRYSANTHEMUM CARE

Dahlias and chrysanthemums come into their true glory at the end of summer and into autumn, just as most flowers have passed their best. Some types are simply left to produce masses of blooms with no intervention, but those grown for large flowers are usually selectively disbudded. This produces fewer but larger blooms. Both types of plant need plenty of feeding and a careful watch has to be kept to prevent pests and diseases marring these plants.

1 To produce larger flowers, pinch out the side buds behind the crown (central) flower bud of dahlias, while they are still small. Many chrysanthemums are also disbudded, but how and when you do it depends on the variety, so be guided by a specialist catalogue or publication.

2 The best way to control pests and diseases is to spray at the first signs. Often it may be possible to prevent spread simply by pinching off and destroying the first few affected leaves. This chrysanthemum shows evidence of leaf miner damage.

3 Chrysanthemums and dahlias benefit from regular feeding. Even if you used a slow-release fertilizer to see them through most of the summer, they will probably respond to a boost now. Use a quick-acting general fertilizer or a high-potash feed, but don't boost with too much nitrogen.

PLANT BULBS FOR SPRING

Spring-flowering bulbs are now widely available, but exactly when you plant them will depend largely on whether the ground has been cleared of summer plants. If planting in beds, it is best to let bedding plants flower for as long as possible, and you may prefer not to disturb the last of the summer color in herbaceous borders just yet, but in vacant ground it is best to plant as soon as possible. Bulbs are always better in the ground rather than in bags and boxes that are probably stored in less than ideal conditions. Bulbs look good in front of shrubs, and you should be able to plant these as soon as they are obtainable. Indoor bulbs that are specially prepared for early flowering should also be planted as soon as they become available.

1 Fork over the ground before planting, and if the plants are to be left undisturbed for some years, try to incorporate plenty of organic material such as rotted garden compost or manure. Many bulbs like well-drained soil but still benefit from plenty of organic material that will hold moisture and nutrients.

2 Avoid adding quick-acting fertilizers in the autumn. Controlled-release fertilizers that provide nutrients according to the soil temperature can be used, but they are best employed in spring. Instead rake a very slow-acting fertilizer such as bonemeal, which contains mainly phosphate, into the surface, or apply it to the planting holes.

3 Where there is space and the plants will benefit from planting in an informal group or cluster, dig out a hole about three times the depth of the bulbs and wide enough to take the clumps.

4 Space the bulbs so that they look like a natural clump. Use the spacing recommended on the packet as a guide. Wide spacing will allow for future growth and multiplication, but if you intend to lift the bulbs after flowering much closer spacing will create a bolder display.

5 Draw the soil back over the bulbs, being careful not to dislodge them in the process.

6 Firm the soil with the back of the rake rather than treading it, which may damage the bulbs.

7 If you are likely to cultivate the area before the shoots come through, mark out where bulbs have been planted with small stakes. Always insert a label, as it will be months before the bulbs appear and flower, by which time it is often difficult to remember the variety planted.

RECOGNIZING WHICH WAY UP TO PLANT BULBS

Most bulbs have a very obvious top and bottom and present no problem. Others, especially tubers, can cause confusion because they lack an obvious growing point. If in doubt, just plant them on their side – the shoot will grow upwards and the roots down.

A few bulbs that do have an obvious top are planted on their side because the base tends to rot in wet soil, though these are rare exceptions. *Fritillaria imperialis* is sometimes planted this way, and it is always worth planting vulnerable bulbs on a bed of grit or coarse sand to encourage good drainage around the base, as shown.

PLANTING IN INDIVIDUAL HOLES

If you have a lot of bulbs to plant over a wide area, individual planting holes may be more appropriate than creating larger excavations to take a group of bulbs.

There are special long-handled planting tools, but an ordinary long-handled trowel is just as good. You can use a normal trowel with a handle of conventional length, but it makes planting more tedious if the area is large.

Check periodically to make sure that the holes are being made to the correct depth. After checking a few it will be easy to judge by eye.

Make a hole large enough to take the bulb easily (it must not become wedged in the hole, as the roots will then be exposed to dry air).

Return the excavated soil. If planting a large area, you can shuffle it back in with your feet, then rake the surface level.

ABOVE: *Tulips, wallflowers and forget-me-nots, all ideal for spring bedding.*

SOW SPRING-FLOWERING POT-PLANTS

Provided you can keep your greenhouse frost-free during the winter – ideally at a minimum of 45°F – it is worth sowing a few flowering plants to bloom next spring. Some suggestions are given in the box below, and those that are hardy, such as calendulas and limnanthes, can even be grown in an unheated greenhouse provided you do not live in a very cold area.

1 As you are only likely to need relatively few plants, sow in pots rather than seed trays. If you don't have a rounded presser to firm the sowing mixture lightly, use the bottom of a jar.

2 Sprinkle the seeds as thinly and evenly as possible over the surface. Large seeds, such as cyclamens, can be spaced individually. Cover with a sprinkling of the sowing mixture if needed (follow the advice on the packet).

3 Stand the pot in a container of water. Letting the moisture seep up from below like this avoids the risk of seeds being washed away or into clumps were you to water the pot from above.

4 Because the outside air temperature is still warm, most seeds will germinate readily without the need for a propagator, but cover with a sheet of glass, or place in a plastic bag, to reduce water loss through evaporation. Seeds that germinate slowly and erratically, such as cyclamen, benefit from being placed in a heated propagator.

SEEDS TO SOW NOW

Browallia
Calendula (choose a very dwarf variety)★
Cineraria
Cyclamen (for home and greenhouse)★★
Exacum affine
Limnanthes douglasii★
Linaria maroccana★
Primula acaulis (cultivated primroses)★
Primula malacoides
Schizanthus

★ These are tough plants that will tolerate some frost and are suitable for an unheated greenhouse in mild areas
★★ Cyclamen should flower in mid winter the following year (ie after about 16 months)

ABOVE: *The pot marigold (*Calendula officinalis*), easy and always cheerful.*

PLANT HYACINTHS FOR EARLY FLOWERING

For early flowering indoors or in the greenhouse, you must choose bulbs that have been 'prepared' or 'treated'. The term may vary, but it simply means that before you receive the bulb it has been stored under specially controlled conditions that make it think more of its resting period has elapsed. It looks no different, but it believes winter is more advanced than in reality and that it needs to grow and bloom quickly.

Ordinary, untreated, hyacinths can be planted now in just the same way, but they will flower later in the season. It is a good idea to pot up some bulbs of both kinds, separately, to spread the flowering period.

1 If using a bowl without drainage, use a special bulb mixture based on peat. If you use a container with drainage holes, any ordinary potting mixture can be used.

2 Place a thin layer of the potting mixture in the container, then space the bulbs close together but make sure they are not touching. An odd number will look better than an even number (three or five bulbs are usually planted in a bowl).

3 Pack more potting mixture around the bulbs, but leave their 'noses' exposed. Water, but be careful not to overwater.

4 Keep the planted bulbs in a cold, dark place indoors, perhaps in the garage, or in a special 'plunge bed' outdoors. Simply stand the bowls in a cool, shady position and cover them with several inches of grit, peat or coarse sand. If the containers lack drainage holes, protect from rain to prevent water-logging. Check the containers for progress periodically.

AUTUMN

Be watchful and vigilant as the nights become colder. In some areas quite severe frosts are common in early autumn, and in others light frosts may not occur until mid or late autumn, if at all. Listen to the weather forecasts and take in or protect vulnerable plants if frost is expected. Think seriously about winter protection for plants on the borderline of hardiness, and be prepared to give early winter shelter, perhaps in the form of a windbreak, for newly planted evergreens. A little protection can ensure that many plants survive instead of succumbing to winter winds and cold.

OPPOSITE: *The colorful leaves of* Rhus typhina *'Laciniata', with the white plumes of a cortaderia in the background.*

ABOVE: Liriope muscari, *one of the delights of autumn, is fortunately tough and very easy to grow.*

EARLY AUTUMN

THE WEATHER IN EARLY AUTUMN IS still warm enough to make outdoor gardening a comfortable experience, and although the vibrant flowers of summer may be gone, there are plenty of delights to be enjoyed in the form of bright berries and flaming foliage, not to mention late-flowering gems such as chrysanthemums and nerines. Apart from bulb planting, and protecting frost-tender plants, there are few really pressing jobs at this time of year.

JOBS IN BRIEF

The kitchen garden

- ☐ Lift onions to store
- ☐ Place cloches over lettuces and other low-growing vegetables that will continue to grow for longer with protection
- ☐ Sow a crop of a green manure (such as buckwheat) to use up nutrients in vacant ground, which will be recycled when the crop is dug in
- ☐ Lift and store maincrop potatoes
- ☐ Protect outdoor tomatoes with cloches or fleece to extend their season and ripen more fruit
- ☐ Summer prune cordon and espalier apples if not already done
- ☐ Clean and store stakes

BELOW: *Extend the vegetable season by covering with cloches.*

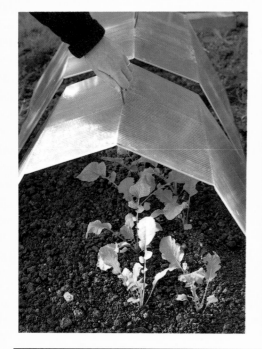

The flower garden

- ☐ Plant spring-flowering bulbs
- ☐ Take fuchsia and pelargonium cuttings
- ☐ Sow hardy annuals to overwinter (only in mild areas or if you can provide winter protection)
- ☐ Plant lilies
- ☐ Clear summer bedding and prepare for spring bedding plants
- ☐ Continue to watch for pests and diseases on roses and other vulnerable plants
- ☐ Disbud dahlias and chrysanthemums as necessary
- ☐ Lift and store dahlias after the first frost
- ☐ Lift and store gladioli and other tender bulbs, corms and tubers
- ☐ Take in tender aquatic plants from the pond if frost is threatened

BELOW: *Tulips are best interplanted with spring bedding plants.*

The greenhouse and conservatory

- ☐ Bring in house and greenhouse plants that have been standing outdoors for the summer
- ☐ Sow spring-flowering plants such as cyclamen, schizanthus and exacums
- ☐ Clean off summer shading washes
- ☐ Repot cacti if they need it
- ☐ Check that greenhouse heaters are in good working order. Arrange to have them serviced, if necessary
- ☐ Pot up and pot on seedling pot-plants as it becomes necessary
- ☐ Plant hyacinths for early flowering under glass

BELOW: *Think about repotting your cacti, a prickly job that has to be done at some time.*

PLANTS AT THEIR BEST

Anemone japonica (herbaceous)
Aster novae-angliae (herbaceous)
Aster novi-belgii (herbaceous)
Chrysanthemum, early-flowering
garden type (herbaceous)
Dahlia (bulb)
Hibiscus syriacus (shrub)
Hydrangea (shrub)
Lavatera (shrub)
Nerine bowdenii (bulb)
Pyracantha, berries (shrub)
Rudbeckia (herbaceous)
Sedum spectabile (herbaceous)
Solidago (herbaceous)
Sorbus, berries (tree)
Sternbergia lutea (bulb)

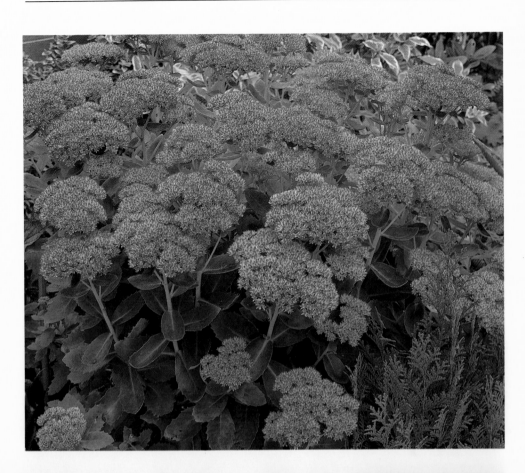

RIGHT: *The autumn-flowering* Sedum
spectabile *is a highlight of autumn.*

BELOW: Rudbeckia fulgida *'Goldstrum' is
one of the stars of the autumn border.*

PUT CLOCHES IN PLACE

If you have cloches that you normally use to protect your crops in spring, make the most of them by extending the end of the season as well as the beginning.

Save large barn cloches for large crops such as tomatoes (see opposite), if wished, and use tent and plastic tunnel cloches for low-growing crops such as lettuces.

1 Winter radishes and daikon radishes are frost-hardy, but you can encourage further growth before bad weather sets in by covering them with cloches. If you failed to sow them earlier, you may be able to start them off under cloches now in a mild area, provided you do so while the soil is still warm.

2 Try sowing lamb's lettuce and winter purslane as a cold month crop. They don't need cloche protection except in cold areas, but the cover will ensure a better supply of more succulent leaves.

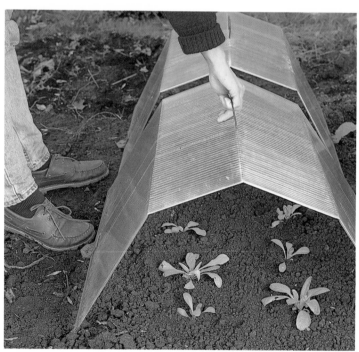

3 Put the cloches in position before the cold weather checks growth. With a little protection like this the plants will crop more freely.

ABOVE: *Put cloches in place now to warm up the soil for early crops such as lettuces.*

RIGHT: *Beets can also be sown earlier if you first warm the soil with cloches.*

PROTECT OUTDOOR TOMATOES

Green tomatoes can be ripened indoors provided they have reached a reasonable stage of maturity, but it makes sense to ripen as many as possible on the plant. As soon as a severe frost is forecast, however, harvest the remaining fruit and ripen as many as possible indoors.

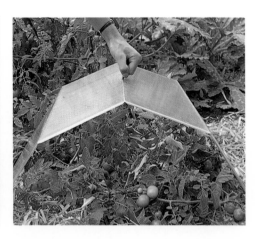

1 Frost will kill tomatoes, but you can often extend their season by a few weeks and ripen a few more fruits on the plant with protection. Bush plants that are already low-growing are best covered with a large cloche. Packing straw beneath the plants first will also provide a little insulation.

2 Cordon-trained tomatoes must be lowered before they can be protected with cloches. Untie the plant and remove the stake.

3 Lay a bed of straw on the ground, then carefully lower the plants onto this. If you lay all the stems in the same direction, you will have a neat row of tomatoes that are easily covered with cloches.

4 Fleece can be used to offer wind protection and enough shelter to keep off a degree or two of frost, though it does not warm the air during the day in the same way as glass or some rigid plastics. Drape several layers over low-growing varieties, and peg it down securely along each side, and at the ends.

5 Fleece can also be used to protect cordon tomatoes while still staked. Sheets of fleece can be wrapped around, or you may be able to buy fleece produced as a tube. Simply cut off the required length, slip it over the plant, and secure at the top and bottom.

PLANT A SPRING WINDOWBOX WITH BULBS

Spring bulb displays are less predictable than summer flowers, and it can be especially disappointing when different bulbs planted in the same windowbox flower at different times. The consolation is that this does at least extend the interest. A good alternative is to plant single-subject displays which, although often brief, are frequently bolder.

1 Make sure that there are drainage holes, and add a layer of material to aid quick drainage, such as broken pots or pieces of chipped bark (sold for mulching).

2 Add enough potting soil to cover the bottom inch or so of the windowbox. As the bulbs do not need a lot of nutrients during the winter, you can often use some of the potting mixture previously used for summer bedding plants.

3 You can pack in more bulbs by planting in layers. Place large bulbs such as daffodils or tulips at the lower level.

4 Add more potting soil, then position the smaller bulbs, such as crocuses and scillas. Try to position them so that they lie between the larger bulbs. Be careful about the bulbs that you mix – small crocuses will be swamped by tall daffodils, so choose miniature or dwarf daffodils, to keep a suitable balance.

5 Finish with more potting soil, but leave ¾–1in of space at the top for watering and perhaps a decorative mulch. As the windowbox will look bare for some months, a few winter pansies will add a touch of interest. Don't worry about the bulbs beneath – they will find their way through the pansies.

BULBS AND SPRING BEDDING

Some of the best container displays for spring combine bulbs with spring-flowering bedding plants such as forget-me-nots (*Myosotis*), double daisies (*Bellis*) and cultivated primroses. This is often more effective than filling the container with bulbs alone. It means that the container looks less bleak after planting, and the period of flowering is greatly extended.

Put the plants in first, then the bulbs between them. If you plant the bulbs first, it will be difficult to remember the positioning and they are likely to be disturbed when you insert the plants.

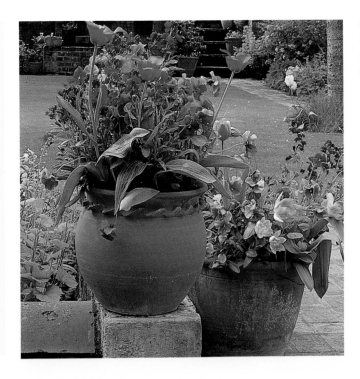

LEFT: *Even common plants like tulips and pansies can look stunning in the right combination and setting.*

PLANT A TUB OR PATIO POT WITH BULBS

Tubs, large pots, and urns can be planted in the same way as windowboxes – with bulbs in multiple layers or combined with spring-flowering plants – but bulbs also make good companions for shrubs and small trees in tubs.

They make the most of space around the edge of the container that is usually wasted, and if the shrubby plant sheds its leaves in winter, the bulbs will complete the important parts of their annual cycle before there is competition · for light.

1 If planting an empty container, try placing a small conifer in the center to provide winter interest. A few ivies positioned so that they trail over the edge will usually improve the appearance in winter.

2 Position the bulbs on the surface first so that they are evenly spaced around the edge. Small plants that multiply freely, such as *Muscari armeniacum*, scillas, chionodoxas, and *Anemone blanda*, are among the plants that can usually be depended upon to improve year by year.

3 Plant with a trowel, being careful to disturb the roots of an established plant as little as possible.

PLANT BEDS AND BORDERS FOR A SPRING DISPLAY

Beds normally used for summer bedding can be replanted with spring bedding – a combination of plants and bulbs will create a better display than bulbs alone. Plants like forget-me-nots and double daisies help to clothe the ground between the bulbs during the winter, and in spring fill in around the base of tall bulbs such as tulips that can otherwise look rather stalky.

It is a good idea to see what your local parks department does for plant combinations. It is better to modify an existing combination that you like, even if you don't want to copy it exactly, rather than experiment if you don't know much about the plants. A failure will mean that you will have to wait another year for the next attempt.

1 Fork over the ground after clearing it of summer bedding plants. Fertilizer is not normally needed, but bonemeal, which is very slow-acting, is worth adding if the soil is impoverished. Apply bonemeal after forking over and rake it in.

2 If you have raised the plants yourself, and have them growing in a nursery bed, water well about an hour before lifting them. Lift with as much soil round the roots as possible.

3 Spring bedding plants bought from garden centers are usually sold in trays or strips. These are usually disposable, so don't be afraid to break them if this allows you to release the root-ball with as little damage as possible.

ABOVE: *Tulips usually look better if underplanted with wallflowers or forget-me-nots.*

4 Space the plants out on the surface, allowing for the bulbs, before planting. Space the bulbs out, then begin planting from the back or one end.

PLANT LILIES FOR SUMMER

Lilies are often planted in spring, but you can also plant them now except in very cold areas. The bulbs are less likely to dry out, which can result in failures. Most lilies prefer a slightly acid soil (pH6–6.5), but some – including *Lilium candidum* – will do well in alkaline soils.

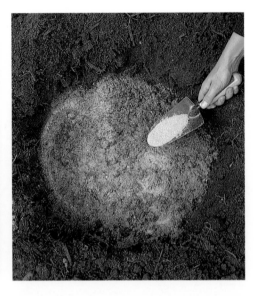

1 Lilies demand a well-prepared site, so dig the soil deeply and work in as much well-rotted manure or garden compost as you can spare. Add plenty of grit to improve drainage if the soil tends to be wet.

2 Lilies look best in groups rather than as isolated specimens, so excavate an area of soil to a depth of about 8in, large enough to take at least four or five bulbs. Add coarse grit or sand unless the soil is very well drained.

3 Add a sprinkling of bonemeal or a controlled-release fertilizer, as lilies are usually left undisturbed until overcrowded and therefore feeding is more important than with bedding bulbs used for a single season.

4 Space the bulbs about 6in apart and make sure that they are deep enough to be covered with about twice their own depth of soil. Sprinkle more grit or coarse sand around the bulbs to deter slugs and reduce the risk of waterlogging.

5 Place small stakes or sticks around the planting area before you return the soil. These remind you to avoid damaging the emerging shoots when you hoe. Remember to label.

ABOVE: *Lilies are real eye-catchers, as this drift of the compact 'Little Girl' proves.*

CLEAR SUMMER BEDDING PLANTS

If frosts have not put an abrupt end to your summer bedding display, the plants will undoubtedly be looking sad and dejected by now.

Even if you do not plan to replant with spring bedding, the garden will look tidier if the old plants are cleared away and the ground dug over.

1 Plants like this will do more good on the compost heap than left on show. Bare soil can look neat and tidy provided you eliminate weeds.

2 Bedding plants generally have shallow roots and are easy to pull up by hand. If some are deep-rooted, just loosen the roots with a fork.

3 Old bedding plants are ideal for the compost heap. Being non-woody they rot down easily.

4 Dig over the ground, and remove any large weeds. Use a spade if the ground is very weedy so that most of them can be buried as the soil is turned, otherwise use a fork.

5 Whether or not you are replanting with spring bedding plants, rake the ground level so that it looks neat and tidy.

PRESERVE AND STORE GARDEN STAKES

Bamboo stakes deteriorate after a season or two in use, especially where they have been in the ground. Extend their life by cleaning and preserving them. Store in a dry place, rather than leaving them exposed in the garden.

1 Knock most of the soil off, then scrub the stakes with a stiff brush and garden or household disinfectant. Pay special attention to the ends, and make sure any soil is removed.

2 Wipe the scrubbed stakes with a cloth to dry them, then stand the ends that have been in the soil in a bucket or container partly filled with a wood preservative. Leave overnight to allow the preservative to penetrate.

3 Bundle the stakes to keep them tidy, and store in a dry place until needed next year.

LIFT AND STORE GLADIOLI

Gladioli can only be left in the ground in mild areas where frosts are always light and do not penetrate far into the soil. In cold areas gladioli will be killed if they remain in the soil, so lift them before there are penetrating frosts.

Gladioli flower reliably from year to year, so they are almost always worth saving. The cormels (small corms) that form around the base will reach flowering size within a couple of years if looked after.

1 Loosen the soil with a garden fork before attempting to lift the plants.

2 Trim off most of the foliage, leaving just a stub to dry off. Shake off most of the soil.

3 Leave the lifted plants in a dry place for a few days to dry off. When the remains of the old stems have shrivelled, trim them off, and remove the cormels that have grown around the base. Store these if you want to save them, otherwise discard. Pull off the remains of the old corm to leave just the healthy new corm. Lay the corms in trays and keep in a frost-proof place for a day or two for further drying.

4 Dust with fungicide and store in paper bags away from frost.

REPOT CACTI AND SUCCULENTS

Cacti and succulents can be repotted at any time of the year, though spring or the end of the growing season are convenient times. Many succulents present no special handling problems, but prickly cacti have to be treated with respect.

If possible, choose a soil mix formulated for cacti, as this will be well drained and have the right sort of structure and nutrient level. A soil-based potting mixture is a practical alternative. Some commercial growers use peat-based potting mixtures, but these are best avoided. Apart from the difficulty in keeping the water balance right, peat-based potting mixtures do not have the weight and structure to support large cacti and succulents.

Large specimens do not need regular repotting. Simply remove about 1in of soil from the top and replace with fresh cactus soil.

1 To handle a prickly cactus, fold a strip of newspaper, thick paper or thin card to make a flexible band that you can wrap around the plant.

2 Tap the pot on a hard surface to loosen the root-ball. You can then often lift the plant out with the improvised handle. If it refuses to move, try pushing a pencil through the drainage hole to break the bond.

3 If the plant has been in the same soil for a long time, crumble away a little of it from the base and around the sides of the root-ball. But be careful to minimize damage to the roots. Just shake off loose soil.

4 The majority of cacti and succulents are best in pots that are quite small in proportion to the size of the top growth. It is usually best to move the plant into a pot only one size larger. If using a clay pot, cover the drainage hole with pieces of broken pot or other material.

5 While holding the plant with the improvised handle, trickle soil mix around the old root-ball. With some cacti, their shape makes this difficult to do without your hand touching the spines, in which case you can use a spoon.

6 Tap the bottom of the pot on a hard surface to settle the soil around the roots. This is especially important as it is often difficult to firm the soil with your fingers if the cactus is prickly. Wait for a couple of days before watering.

BRING IN POT-PLANTS FROM THE GARDEN

Many winter and spring-flowering houseplants, such as schulmbergeras, zygocactus, and solanums grown for their winter berries, even orchids, can spend the summer outdoors as they look uninteresting at this stage. Make sure these are brought in before the first frost threatens.

1 Clear away the mulching material if the pots have been plunged into the ground and mulched to reduce the need for regular watering.

2 If the pots do not come up easily, insert a garden fork a little distance away and lever them gently to avoid damaging the pots.

3 Remove leaves and debris from the surface of the potting soil, which will almost certainly have become contaminated. Wipe the pot clean with a damp cloth, and be especially careful to clean the bottom of the pot so that it does not make a mess indoors.

4 Always check for pests and diseases before taking the plant indoors or into the greenhouse. Look on the backs of the leaves too, which is where snails will often be found. Even a small snail can do a lot of damage if left undetected. If the plant has thick or glossy leaves, wipe them over with a ready-made leaf shine to improve their appearance. Plants left outdoors almost always become splashed with mud and dirt.

GREENHOUSE SHADING

Plants now need all the light they can get, so remove greenhouse shading as soon as possible. If you applied a shading wash earlier in the year, clean it off now. Most can be rubbed off with a duster when the glass is dry. Internal or external shading material such as blinds or nets can also be removed now, as shown here. You may be able to use the same internal fixings to secure winter insulation.

MID AUTUMN

THIS IS AN UNPREDICTABLE TIME OF the year. In cold regions quite severe frosts are not uncommon, while in mild climates some plants are still growing and tender plants may not be brought to an abrupt end for another month or more. This is a time to listen to the weather forecast and to be on the alert, in particular, for frost warnings if you haven't yet had the first frost. Be flexible and garden with an eye to the weather as well as the calendar.

JOBS IN BRIEF

The kitchen garden

- ☐ Plant cabbages for spring harvesting
- ☐ Thin late-sown lettuces for winter harvesting
- ☐ Continue to earth up celery and leeks
- ☐ Lift and store potatoes
- ☐ Protect late cauliflowers from frost by bending surrounding leaves over the heads
- ☐ Cut the dead tops off asparagus
- ☐ Use cloches to protect vulnerable vegetables
- ☐ Start winter digging on heavy soils
- ☐ Pot up some herbs for winter use
- ☐ Pick and store apples when ready
- ☐ Take black currant cuttings
- ☐ Prune black currants, gooseberries and raspberries
- ☐ Cover late-fruiting strawberries with cloches to extend the season
- ☐ Plant bare-root fruit bushes and trees
- ☐ Apply greasebands to apple trees

BELOW: *Greasebanding is a non-chemical method of controlling some fruit pests.*

The flower garden

- ☐ Make a new lawn from turf
- ☐ Give an established lawn autumn lawncare treatment
- ☐ Plant roses
- ☐ Plant bare-root and balled trees and shrubs
- ☐ Plant herbaceous plants
- ☐ Divide over-large herbaceous plants
- ☐ Clear summer bedding plants
- ☐ Plant spring bulbs
- ☐ Take in tender fuchsias and pelargoniums
- ☐ Protect vulnerable plants

BELOW: *Bare-root plants can be dug in temporarily if you are not ready to plant.*

- ☐ Cut down and lift dahlias blackened by frost
- ☐ Lift and take in chrysanthemums not hardy enough to overwinter outside
- ☐ Lift gladioli corms
- ☐ Plant lilies
- ☐ Sow sweet peas in pots
- ☐ Plant hedges
- ☐ Prepare the pond for winter
- ☐ Collect and compost fallen leaves
- ☐ Remove leaves that have fallen on rock plants

The greenhouse and conservatory

- ☐ Clean and disinfect, ready for winter
- ☐ Insulate
- ☐ Remove yellowing and dead leaves from plants – pick them off the pot as well as the plant
- ☐ Check that heaters are working properly
- ☐ Check minimum temperatures being achieved (if you don't have a minimum-maximum thermometer, buy one)
- ☐ Ventilate whenever the weather is mild enough

BELOW: *Bubble insulation will save money if you heat your greenhouse in winter.*

PLANTS AT THEIR BEST

Acer, colorful foliage (tree/shrub)
Anemone japonica (herbaceous)
Aster novi-belgii (herbaceous)
Berberis, colorful foliage and berries (shrub)
Fothergilla, colorful foliage (shrub)
Liriope muscari (herbaceous)
Parthenocissus, colorful foliage (climber)
Pernettya, berries (shrub)
Pyracantha, berries (shrub)
Schizostylis coccinea (herbaceous)

LEFT: *Apples are very decorative fruits, and some will be ready to harvest.*

BELOW LEFT: Parthenocissus tricuspidatus *ends its season with brilliant autumn color.*

BELOW: *'Audrey' is one of many varieties of* Aster novi-belgii, *ideal for autumn color.*

LIFT AND STORE POTATOES

Early and mid-season varieties are best eaten soon after harvesting, but the late varieties are grown mainly for storing for winter use. If you grow a small quantity they are best stored in paper sacks kept indoors, but if you grow a lot and indoor storage space is limited, try using the traditional clamping method. It looks primitive but works except where winters are very severe.

1 Lift the tubers with a fork once the foliage has died down. You can leave them in the ground for longer if penetrating frosts are not likely to be a problem, but lift promptly if pests like slugs appear.

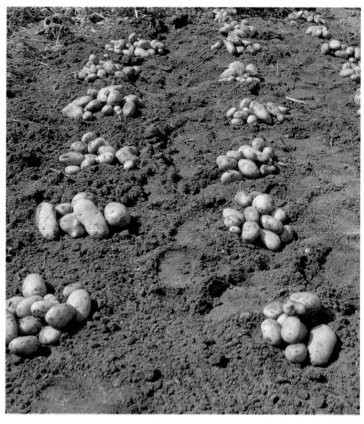

2 Leave the potatoes on the surface for a couple of hours so that the skins dry off and harden.

3 Sort the potatoes before storing. It is sufficient to grade them into four sizes: very small, small, medium and large. Discard or use up very small ones immediately, keep small ones for use soon, and only store the medium and largest.

RIGHT: *Potatoes are best left to dry off for a couple of hours before sorting and storing.*

4 Place the largest potatoes in sacks to store in a cool but frost-proof place. Paper sacks are best, but if you can't obtain them, use plastic sacks in which case make slits with a knife to provide some ventilation.

5 If you have too many potatoes to store in sacks, or don't have space indoors, make a clamp in the garden. Excavate a shallow depression and line it with a thick layer of straw.

6 Pile the potatoes on to the bed of straw, as shown.

7 Heap a thick layer of straw over the top. It must be thick enough to provide good insulation.

8 Mound earth over the straw, but leave a few tufts of straw sticking out of the top for ventilation.

PROLONGING HERBS

Parsley is one of the herbs that will continue to provide leaves for harvesting throughout the winter if you protect the plants with cloches. Make sure that the end pieces are tightly secured.

STRAW PROTECTION

Vegetables such as celery (shown here) and beets benefit in cold areas if you protect the stems with straw. Pack the straw among and between the plants in the blocks or rows. It does not matter if the tops of the leaves are exposed – you are only protecting the edible part.

Mature celery will usually survive some frost, but the protection is useful if it turns very cold before you are ready to lift it. In mild areas you can leave beets unprotected, but the straw packing does help to keep plants in better condition for longer in cold areas.

NATURALIZE BULBS IN GRASS

Naturalizing bulbs is a good way to enjoy a trouble-free display each spring, and one that should improve each year. You will need an area of grass that you don't mind leaving unmown until early summer, to allow bulb foliage to die back naturally.

1 If you have a lot of small bulbs, such as crocuses and eranthis, to plant in a limited area, try lifting an area of turf. Use a spade or half-moon edger to make an H-shaped cut.

2 Slice beneath the grass with a spade until you can fold the turf back for planting.

3 Loosen the ground first, as it will be very compacted. If you want to apply a slow-acting fertilizer such as bonemeal, work it into the soil at the same time.

4 Avoid planting in rows or regimented patterns. You want them to look natural and informal, so scatter them and plant where they fall.

5 If you plant large bulbs this way, you will have to make deeper holes with a trowel. Plant them so that they are covered with about twice their own depth of soil.

6 Firm the soil then return the grass. Firm again if necessary to make sure it is flat, and water if the weather is dry to ensure that the grass grows again quickly.

7 Large bulbs such as daffodils are easier to plant using a bulb planter that takes out a core of soil. Scatter the bulbs randomly so that the display will look natural.

8 Push the bulb planter into the soil, twisting it a little if the ground is hard, then pull it out with the core of soil. Release the core of soil and place the bulb at the bottom of the hole.

9 First pull off a little soil from the base of the core (to allow for the depth of the bulb), then replace the core in the hole. Firm gently.

RIGHT: *Try naturalizing bulbs, like these anemones, at the edge of the lawn, where you can leave the grass long until the plants die down.*

LIFT AND STORE DAHLIAS

Do not discard your dahlias – lift the tubers before frosts penetrate the ground, and store them for next year. Even seed-raised plants will have formed tubers that you can store.

1 Lift the dahlia tubers once the first frosts have blackened the foliage. Use a fork to lift the tubers, to minimize the risk of damaging them. Cut off the old stem to leave a stump about 2in long.

2 Stand the tubers upside down so that moisture drains easily from the hollow stems. Using a mesh support is a convenient way to allow them to dry off. Keep in a dry, frost-free place.

3 After a few days the tubers should be dry enough to store. Remove surplus soil, trim off loose bits of old roots and shorten the stem to leave a short stump. Label each plant.

4 Pack the tubers in a well-insulated box with peat, vermiculite, wood shavings, or crumpled newspaper placed between them. Keep in a frost-free location.

WINTER QUARTERS

A spare bedroom or cool but frost-free garage are sensible places to store overwintering bulbs, corms and tubers such as dahlias. Avoid a very warm place, as roots will spread more rapidly if they become established, and the bulbs or tubers are more likely to dry out. Keep bulbs, corms and tubers where you can easily check them about once a month, to ensure they are all still sound. Any that start to rot must be removed immediately.

PREPARE THE POND FOR WINTER

Although ponds need little routine maintenance, there are a few end-of-season tasks that are essential if you want to keep your plants and fish in good condition.

1 Protect the pond from the worst of the leaf fall with a fine-mesh net. Anchor it just above the surface of the pond. This is not practical for a large pond, but it is useful for a small one. Remove the leaves regularly, and eventually take the netting off.

2 If you are not able to cover your pond with a net, or don't like the appearance of one, use a fish net or rake to remove leaves regularly – not only from the surface, but also from below the surface as well. Too many leaves in the water can pollute the pond.

3 Submerged oxygenating plants, such as elodea and rampant growers like myriophyllum, will eventually clog the pond unless you net or rake them out periodically. This is a good time to thin them simply by raking out the excess.

4 Trim back dead or dying plants from around the edge of the pond, especially where the vegetation is likely to fall into the water.

5 To divide overgrown water plants, first remove the plants from their containers. It may be necessary to cut some roots to do so.

6 Some plants can simply be pulled apart by hand, but others will have such a tight mass of entangled roots that you need to chop them into smaller pieces with a spade.

7 Discard any pieces you don't want for replanting, then pot up the others in planting baskets. Cover the top of the baskets with gravel to prevent soil disturbance.

TAKE IN TENDER AQUATICS

Some aquatic plants, such as the water lettuce (*Pistia stratiotes*) and *Salvinia auriculata*, will be killed by frost, even though they can multiply rapidly outdoors in summer. The fairy moss (*Azolla caroliniana*) sometimes survives a mild winter in favorable areas, but as an insurance policy a few plants should be overwintered in a frost-proof place.

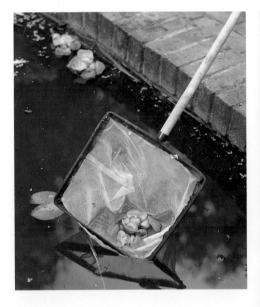

1 Net a few plants in good condition. They may already be deteriorating in the cooler weather, so don't save any that appear to be rotting or badly damaged.

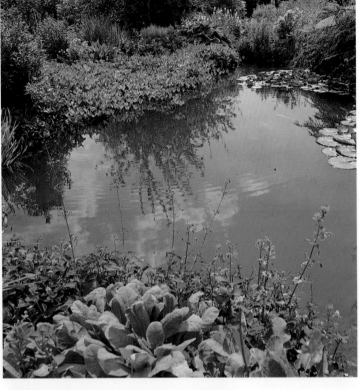

LEFT: *A pond can look perfect in summer, but if you have tender pond plants, now is the time to take them in.*

2 Put a handful of the plants into a plastic container – such as a lunch box or ice cream container. Don't cram them in so that they are overcrowded. Use extra containers rather than have them all touching. Some gardeners put a little soil in the bottom to provide nutrients.

3 Keep the plants in a warm, light place, such as a greenhouse. You might also be able to keep them on a light windowsill. Top up or change the water occasionally to prevent the water becoming stagnant.

CARING FOR MINIATURE WATERLILIES

With the exception of tropical waterlilies, which are usually only grown by enthusiasts with heated pools, waterlilies are very hardy and are usually planted deep enough not to come to any harm.

Miniature waterlilies are sometimes used for raised miniature pools, in a half barrel or shrub tub for example, and these are vulnerable. Because the container is raised above the ground, in very severe weather the water can freeze solid throughout. This can lead to winter losses. Try wrapping your raised miniature pool in several layers of bubble insulation material, or move it into a cool greenhouse for the winter.

Autumn Lawncare

Autumn is a good time to prepare your lawn for the year ahead, and the best time to tackle any long-term improvements. Tasks, such as raking out lawn debris, eradicating moss, feeding and aerating, will improve the quality of your lawn greatly if carried out on a yearly basis.

1 Over the years, grass clippings and debris form a 'thatch' on the surface of your lawn. This affects growth of the grass and should be removed with a lawn rake. Raking also removes moss.

2 If grass growth is poor, aerate the lawn. You can do this by pushing the prongs of a fork about 6in into the ground.

3 Brush a soil improver into the holes made by the fork. Use sand or a mixture of fine soil and sand if the ground is poorly drained. Alternatively, use peat, a peat–substitute, or very fine, well-rotted compost if the ground is sandy.

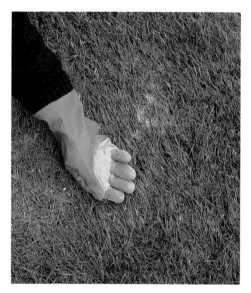

4 If your lawn is in poor condition and needs reviving, apply an autumn lawn feed. It is essential that you use one formulated for autumn use, as spring and summer feeds will contain too much nitrogen.

5 If the grass contains a lot of moss, apply a moss killer. Use one recommended for autumn use – the mixture known as lawn sand, sometimes used to kill moss, contains too much nitrogen.

6 You can tidy an uneven edge at any time, but doing it in autumn will relieve the pressure at busier times of year. Hold a half-moon edger against a board held in position with your feet. This is not an annual job.

COLLECT AND COMPOST LEAVES

Never waste leaves: they will make excellent garden compost if you rot them down; and, if left on the ground, they can damage areas of grass and smother small plants.

1 Don't let leaves lie for long on your lawn. The grass beneath will turn yellow and be prone to disease. On a small lawn, rake them up with a lawn rake.

2 Leaves on paths and drives are best brushed up with a broom or besom.

4 Leaves can be added to the compost heap or bin, but some leaves rot down slowly, so it is best to compost a large amount on their own. Rotted leaves are a useful addition to potting soils.

3 You can buy special tools to lift the leaves without too much bending, but two pieces of wood are also an effective way to lift them once they have been brushed into a heap.

MECHANICAL AIDS

Raking out thatch and moss from your lawn by hand is tiring. If you have a large lawn, invest in a powered lawn rake. This will do the job rapidly and efficiently. Take the drudgery out of aerating your lawn by using a hollow-tined aerator that removes a core of soil effortlessly and efficiently. Equally, you could invest in a powered lawn rake or a special leaf sweeper to clear large lawns of leaves.

DON'T LET LEAVES SMOTHER SMALL PLANTS

If you let leaves lie for long on small plants, such as alpines, they may begin to rot due to the lack of light and free movement of air. The leaves will also provide a haven for slugs and other pests that may eat your plants. Wait until most of the leaves have fallen from the trees, then go around and pick them off vulnerable plants, as shown.

PROTECT VULNERABLE SHRUBS

Many shrubs on the borderline of hardiness can be coaxed through the winter with a little protection. There are several methods you can use to provide shelter.

1 A little protection from cold winds and snow is all that many cold-sensitive shrubs require in areas where they are of borderline hardiness. Push cut branches of evergreens, such as conifers, into the soil around the plant.

2 If the shrub is tall, you may also need to tie cut branches of evergreens, or bracken, so that they remain in position.

3 If you don't have a supply of evergreen shoots or bracken, use horticultural fleece or a woven mesh for protection. For extra protection, fold these over to give more than one thickness before tying into position.

4 Some shrubs are damaged by cold winds as much as low temperatures, and for these a windbreak will prevent wind scorch. Insert stakes around the plant, then fix several layers of wind-break netting or plastic sheeting to these.

RIGHT: *Always knock heavy falls of snow off your conifers before the weight can damage the branches and spoil the shape of the tree.*

PROTECT NEWLY PLANTED EVERGREENS

An evergreen planted in late summer or the autumn may not have grown new roots out into the soil, and if not watered regularly, it will not be able to absorb water as rapidly as it is lost. A windbreak for the first winter will reduce moisture loss and help a vulnerable plant to survive.

2 If you don't want to erect a shield, perhaps on aesthetic grounds, water in very dry spells to keep the roots moist, and cover the plant with a large plastic bag, pegged to the ground, when very severe weather is forecast. Remove it afterwards.

1 Insert three stout stakes around the plant, then wrap a plastic sheet or several layers of horticultural fleece around the edge. Peg down the bottom to secure.

PROTECT DELICATE ALPINES

Some alpines with hairy leaves are likely to rot if they become too wet and waterlogged during the cold months.

SNOW PROTECTION

1 If you know that a particular alpine needs winter wet protection, cover it with a sheet of glass or rigid plastic substitute supported on special wires.

2 You can also use bricks to support and weight the pane. If you have a spare cloche, perhaps not needed until spring, you might be able to use this to protect alpines. Leave the ends open, but make sure that the cloche is firmly anchored and not likely to be lifted by strong winds.

Conifers with an attractive or formal shape can be disfigured by a heavy fall of snow that pulls down or breaks the branches. If you live in an area of heavy snowfall, tie the branches, as shown. Green or brown twine is less conspicuous than string.

PLANT A HEDGE

Shrubs can be planted at almost any time of the year if you buy them in containers, but this is an expensive way to plant a hedge as you need so many plants. Most garden centers stock bundles of bare-root hedging plants at this time, so plant now if you want to create a hedge economically.

1 Prepare the ground thoroughly, as a hedge will be there for a long time and this is your only opportunity to improve the soil. Clear it of weeds, and dig deeply, especially if the soil is shallow or compacted.

2 Open up a trench about 10in deep, using a garden line to ensure that the row will be straight.

3 Add as much garden compost or rotted manure as you can spare, then fork it into the base of the trench to improve the soil and encourage deep rooting.

4 Return the soil to the trench, adding more organic material as you do so. Then apply bonemeal and rake it in. Don't apply fast-acting fertilizers at this time of year.

5 You may find bare-root hedging simply bundled together, with their roots in a bed of peat or soil. If not, and if you will not be planting it out immediately, dig the hedging into a spare piece of ground.

6 Dig large holes at the appropriate spacing. A typical spacing is 15–18in, but it may be different for some plants, so always check the recommended spacing first.

7 Firm the plants in well, treading around them to remove any large air pockets that may cause the roots to dry out.

8 Water thoroughly, and be prepared to water regularly in dry spells for the first year.

PLANT A ROSE

Nowadays roses get planted throughout the year because most are grown in containers. Those ordered from specialist nurseries by mail order may arrive bare-root, however, and some garden centers and other stores also sell them like this in the autumn, perhaps with their roots wrapped in moss and a protective sleeve. These are plants that have been lifted from the field; they are often less expensive than those grown in containers, and can be just as good if planted promptly.

PLANTING A CLIMBING ROSE

Never plant a climbing rose too close to a wall or fence. Try to position the root-ball about 15in away, and angle the stem slightly towards the support. In this way, the shoots can be trained normally, yet the roots will not be in the driest area of soil.

LEFT: *Roses always add charm to a garden, and now is a good time to plant.*

1 Dig a hole large enough to spread all the roots out, and fork in as much garden compost or rotted manure as you can spare. It is especially important to break up any compacted soil.

2 Trim off any broken or damaged roots, and if they appear dry, soak the roots in a bucket of water for an hour or two.

3 Trickle soil back around the roots, remembering to give the plant a shake occasionally to settle the soil around them.

4 To ensure the rose is planted firmly, with no large pockets of air, and that the bush cannot be rocked by wind, firm the soil with your feet. Rake over and water thoroughly.

5 If the plant was unpruned when bought, cut back all the shoots to about 6–8in) above the ground. This will also reduce the risk of winds loosening the rose.

INSULATE THE GREENHOUSE

Insulation will cut down heating costs. Even if you don't heat your greenhouse during the winter, insulation will afford extra protection for those not-quite-hardy plants.

1 There are many ready-made fasteners for securing polyethylene to the inside of a metal greenhouse. They usually slot into the groove in the metal molding and can be secured in position with a twisting motion.

2 With the main part of the clip in place, the top is pushed or twisted into position, clamping the polyethylene liner. If using thick bubble polyethylene, you may need clips designed for the extra thickness.

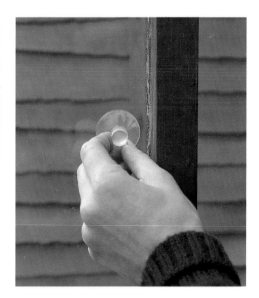

3 You may find it easier to line the sides and roof separately. If you decide to do this, be prepared to use a draught proofing strip if there is a gap at the eaves.

4 You can fix the insulation to a timber-framed greenhouse with drawing pins, or special pins sold for the purpose.

5 If you don't want to fix the insulation directly to the wooden frame, suction fixers can be attached to the glass. These can also be used for metal-framed greenhouses. Moisten the plastic before pressing into place.

7 Whichever method of fixing you choose, you should always insulate the ventilators separately. Although you need to conserve heat as much as possible, some ventilation is essential when it's warm enough. You must be able to open at least one ventilator if necessary.

6 Secure the liner to the cup with the special pin provided (or use a drawing pin).

8 To avoid too much warmth being lost between the sheets where they join, seal joins with a transparent tape.

RIGHT: *Bubble insulation will keep the temperature up and your bills down.*

SCREENS AND DIVIDERS

Thermal screens made of clear plastic or special translucent fabrics are widely used commercially to conserve heat. Fixed horizontally over the plants, they seal off the space at the top of the greenhouse. They are usually pulled across at night, and drawn back during the day. A similar technique can be used in your own greenhouse by stretching supporting wires along each side of the greenhouse, over which the fabric can be draped or pulled (see below left).

If you have a large greenhouse, it may be more economic to heat just part of it. Use a vertical screen to partition off the end (see below right) to reduce the area to be heated.

INSULATION MATERIALS

Proper double glazing is not very practical or cost-effective for most amateur greenhouses where very high temperatures are not normally maintained. Polyethylene sheeting is the most practical choice as it can be taken down at the end of the heating season and used again if stored carefully for the summer.

Single thickness, heavy-duty polyethylene lets through plenty of light, and is cheap to buy, but it is not the most effective material for conserving heat.

Bubble polyethylene is more efficient because air trapped in the bubbles cuts down heat loss. If possible, choose bubble polyethylene that is thick, with large pockets of air. It lets through less light, but is more efficient at reducing heat loss.

OVERWINTER TENDER FUCHSIAS

Most fuchsias are killed by frost, so unless you know that a particular variety is hardy enough to be left outdoors for the winter in your area, overwinter them in a frost-proof place.

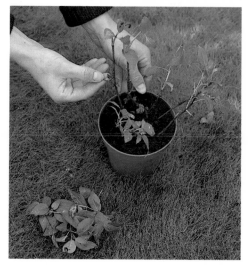

1 If your fuchsias have been grown in pots during the summer, lift them to take into the greenhouse. If planted in the open soil, lift with a fork and remove excess soil.

2 Pot up the plants individually, or in large boxes if you have a lot of plants, then put them in a frost-free place, such as in the greenhouse or on a light windowsill indoors.

3 Tidy up the plants by removing old leaves and pinching out any soft green tips. You must keep the plants cool but frost-free, with the soil almost dry.

OVERWINTERING FUCHSIAS OUTDOORS

If you don't have a greenhouse or space indoors, try this method instead of throwing the plants away. Dig a trench about 12in deep, line with straw, then lay the plants on this, as shown above. Cover the plants with more straw and then return the soil.

Dig them up in spring, pot them up and keep in warmth and good light to start into growth again. If the winters are not too harsh, many of the plants should survive.

PROTECTING HARDY FUCHSIAS

Hardy is a relative term, and although some fuchsias are tough enough for the roots not to be killed by frost where winters are not too severe, in cold areas they may succumb without a little extra protection.

Leave the old stems on, even though these will be killed, as this may afford the plant some additional shelter. To reduce the depth to which severe frosts penetrate, cover the crown with a thick layer of bracken, straw or peat, as shown here. Remove the protection in spring when the new shoots appear.

In mild areas, extra protection is not necessary for tough species such as *Fuchsia magellanica*.

OVERWINTER PELARGONIUMS

Pelargoniums, otherwise known as bedding geraniums, should be overwintered in a light and frost-free environment. If you have a lot of plants, a greenhouse is the best place to keep them, but if you do not have a greenhouse you may have space for a few plants indoors.

1 Lift the plants before the first frost if possible, though they will often survive a light frost if you take them in promptly afterwards.

2 Shake as much of the soil off the roots as possible, to reduce the size of the plant.

3 Trim the longest roots back to about 2–3in long, to make potting up easier.

4 Shorten the shoots to about 4in, and trim off any remaining leaves. Although this looks drastic, new shoots will grow in spring, which you can use for cuttings if you want more plants.

6 If you want to overwinter your pelargoniums on a windowsill indoors, you may find it more convenient to use large pots instead of trays.

5 The most effective way to store pelargoniums for the winter is in large trays at least 6in deep. Half fill with soil or a sowing mixture, position the plants and add more soil mix to cover the roots. Water well initially, then only when the soil becomes almost dry.

DEALING WITH YOUNG PLANTS

Fuchsias and pelargoniums can be rooted from cuttings taken in spring or autumn. If you are overwintering old plants, you can use them to provide plenty of cuttings in spring.

If you took cuttings in late summer or the autumn, however, your young plants will still be growing actively. Make sure that you keep these plants in good light and reasonably warm, in which case they will probably retain their foliage. If conditions are favorable, pelargoniums may even flower during the winter months.

LATE AUTUMN

A LAST-MINUTE SPURT OF ACTION IS often needed at this time of year, to get the garden ready for winter and ensure protection for plants that need it. In cold areas winter will already have taken its grip, but in warmer climates there are still many mild days to be enjoyed. Take advantage of them before colder temperatures and strong winds drive you indoors.

JOBS IN BRIEF

The kitchen garden

- ☐ Protect late cauliflowers from frost by bending surrounding leaves over the head
- ☐ Use cloches to protect vulnerable vegetables
- ☐ Winter dig, especially heavy soils
- ☐ Pot up some herbs for winter use
- ☐ Prune black currants, gooseberries and raspberries
- ☐ Plant bare-root fruit bushes and trees

BELOW: *Pot up a few mint roots to prolong the season and for early leaves next spring.*

The flower garden

- ☐ Cut down the dead tops of herbaceous perennials
- ☐ Get rid of garden refuse by composting
- ☐ Remove pumps from the pond and store for the winter
- ☐ Plant roses
- ☐ Plant bare-root and balled trees and shrubs
- ☐ Clear summer bedding plants if not already done so
- ☐ Finish planting spring bulbs as soon as possible
- ☐ Protect vulnerable plants that will remain in the garden
- ☐ Lift and take in chrysanthemums not hardy enough to overwinter outside
- ☐ Take hardwood shrub cuttings
- ☐ Plant hedges
- ☐ Prepare the pond for winter
- ☐ Collect and compost fallen leaves
- ☐ Remove leaves that have fallen on rock plants
- ☐ Cover alpines that need protection from winter wet with a pane of glass
- ☐ Protect the crowns of vulnerable herbaceous plants such as delphiniums and lupines from slugs by sprinkling coarse grit around them

The greenhouse and conservatory

- ☐ Clean and disinfect, ready for winter
- ☐ Insulate
- ☐ Check the minimum temperatures being achieved (if you don't have a minimum-maximum thermometer, buy one)
- ☐ Ventilate whenever the weather is mild enough
- ☐ Except with winter-flowering plants that are still in strong, active growth, gradually give plants less water. Most will then tolerate low temperatures better and disease should be less of a problem

BELOW: *This is a good time to wash and scrub all those dirty pots.*

PLANTS AT THEIR BEST

Acer, colorful foliage (tree/shrub)
Berberis, colorful foliage and berries (shrub)
Cotoneaster, berries (shrub)
Fothergilla, colorful foliage (shrub)
Gentiana sino-ornata (alpine)
Liriope muscari (herbaceous)
Nerine bowdenii (bulb)
Pernettya, berries (shrub)
Pyracantha, berries (shrub)
Schizostylis coccinea (herbaceous)

LEFT: *Forthergillas are uninspiring for most of the year, with white flowers in late spring and early summer, but in autumn they take center stage with brilliant leaf coloring.*

BELOW: Schizostylis coccinea *is always an eye-catcher in late autumn, when most other border plants have finished flowering.*

PRUNE BLACK CURRANTS

Black currants fruit best on year-old branches, so in pruning an established bush the aim is to remove the oldest shoots and encourage new ones. Prune while the plant is dormant.

1 Only start pruning once they are old enough to fruit reliably. Cut back one-third of the shoots close to the base, choosing the oldest.

2 Cut back to their point of origin any diseased, damaged or badly placed shoots.

3 This is what the bush should look like after pruning, with plenty of well-spaced young shoots.

PRUNE RED AND WHITE CURRANTS

Unlike black currants, these fruit on shoots that are at least two years old. They are usually grown on a 'leg' (a short length of clear stem) as shown, but can be grown as a bush or trained as cordons.

1 If it was not done in the summer, start by removing any crossing or over-crowded shoots, to allow plenty of light into the center of the bush.

2 When badly placed shoots have been removed, shorten last summer's growth at the tip of each main shoot by half.

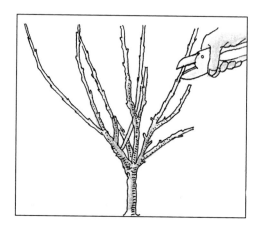

3 Finally, cut back the side-shoots to within one or two buds of the main stems. This will encourage fruiting.

4 On an old bush it may be necessary to cut out a few very old shoots that no longer fruit well, but try to leave a vigorous young sideshoot to replace each one.

PRUNE RASPBERRIES

Autumn-fruiting raspberries bear fruit on canes grown that year, so pruning is easy. Summer-fruiting raspberries fruit on shoots that are a year old, so be careful not to prune last summer's shoots.

1 Provided you are sure the variety is autumn-fruiting, simply cut all the canes down to ground level while they are dormant.

2 On summer-fruiting raspberries cut the old canes (dark stems) that fruited this summer to just above the ground. Tie in the remaining shoots to support wires if necessary.

3 If the raspberries have been growing undisturbed for several years, the clumps may have become congested. Thin out surplus canes to leave them about 3in apart.

PRUNE GOOSEBERRIES

Gooseberries fruit on shoots that are a year or more old, and continue to fruit quite well even if you neglect pruning. But with spiny stems, the fruit is difficult to harvest if not pruned annually.

1 If the job was not done after harvesting, cut out any low branches near the soil to an upward-pointing bud, and also eliminate any badly placed and crossing branches. Try to ensure that the center of the bush is left open.

2 While the bush is dormant, reduce the length of new summer growth at the tips of the main shoots by about half. Then go along each main branch and prune back the sideshoots to two buds from the old wood.

3 If the plant is old, cut out one or two of the oldest shoots, to a point where there is a younger replacement to take over.

PLANT SOFT FRUIT

Nowadays most soft fruits – with the exception of cane plants such as raspberries – are usually sold in containers. They can be planted at almost any time, but late autumn is ideal when there is a good choice of plants in garden centers. Bare-root plants must be planted while dormant.

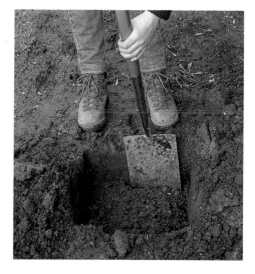

1 Excavate the soil for an area at least twice the size of the root-ball or container so that you can improve the soil over an area that the roots are likely to explore later.

2 Although it is not essential, your fruit will do much better if you can add plenty of humus-making material to the soil. Dig in as much rotten manure or garden compost as you can spare.

3 Soak the roots of bare-root plants in water for an hour before planting, and water container-grown plants for at least half an hour before planting. Place a plant in the hole and use a stake to make sure that it will be at its original depth.

4 Firm the plant in well, pressing with the heel of the foot to remove any large pockets of air around the roots.

5 After firming the soil, hoe and rake the ground to remove footprints, then water thoroughly.

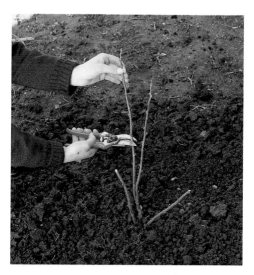

6 Although it seems drastic, most bushes grown on stems that sprout from the base, such as black currants and raspberries, are best cut back to about 9–12in after planting. This will stimulate new shoots to grow from the base.

POT UP HERBS FOR WINTER USE

You don't have to make do with dried or frozen herbs just because it is winter. Some herbs, such as mint, chives, parsley and marjoram, can be potted up to grow indoors or in the greenhouse for a fresh supply of winter leaves. The supply will be modest, but no less welcome.

1 Mint is an easy plant to force indoors, or in a cold frame or greenhouse. Lift an established clump to provide a supply of roots to pot up.

2 Be careful to select only pieces with healthy leaves (diseased leaves are common by the end of the season). You can pull pieces off by hand or cut through them with a knife.

3 Plant the roots in a pot if you want to try to keep the plant growing indoors for a month or so longer. Three-quarters fill an 8–10in pot with soil or potting soil, then spread the roots out and cover with more soil.

4 If you want a supply of tender fresh leaves early next spring, cut off the tops and put the roots in seed trays or deeper boxes, then cover them with soil. If you keep them in a greenhouse (or even a protected cold frame) you will be able to harvest new mint much earlier.

5 Chives also respond favorably to lifting for an extended season. Lift a small clump to pot up. If it's too large, you should be able to pull it apart into smaller pieces.

6 Place the clump in a pot of ordinary garden soil or potting soil, firm well, and water thoroughly. It should continue to provide leaves after those outdoors have died back, and will produce new ones earlier next spring.

PARSLEY AND MARJORAM

If you cut down and pot up marjoram, it will usually spring into new growth provided warmth and light are right.

Parsley is always a dependable winter herb if grown from a late summer or autumn sowing and kept on a windowsill.

LIFT AND PROTECT CHRYSANTHEMUMS

Not all autumn-flowering chrysanthemums have to be lifted (see box), but many do. The roots are potted into boxes, which means that you can start them off in warmth in spring.

2 Shake surplus soil off the roots before removing from the garden.

1 Lift the roots after the plants have finished flowering and before severe frosts arrive.

3 Trim the tops off and cut any long, straggly roots back to keep the root-ball compact.

4 Place a layer of soil or potting soil in a box or tray about 4in deep. Position the roots and cover them with about 1in of soil, firming lightly. Don't forget to label the plants. Keep the box in a cool, light place, such as a cool greenhouse, light garage windowsill, or a cold frame. For most types of chrysanthemum it does not matter if they receive a touch of frost. Keep the soil slightly damp but not wet.

BELOW: Chrysanthemum *'Countryman', is a reflexed early-flowering outdoor variety*.

OVERWINTERING CHRYSANTHEMUMS

There are many kinds of chrysanthemum, but it is only the autumn-flowering chrysanthemums that are likely to cause confusion regarding overwintering.

In mild, frost-free climates they can all be left in the ground, and many of the species like *Chrysanthemum rubellum*, are hardy even in cold areas.

But in temperate climates the highly bred early-flowering autumn chrysanthemums are best lifted and stored, and even those outdoor ones that flower later are best treated this way. Even those that tolerate some frost are more likely to survive if kept fairly dry. Wet and cold is the combination to avoid.

PROTECT POND PUMPS

If you leave a pump in your pond over winter, ice may damage it. Don't just take it out of the pond and leave it where moisture can enter – store it in a dry place.

1 Remove submersible pumps from the water before penetrating frosts cause the water to freeze deeply.

2 Clean the pump before you put it away. It will probably be covered with algae which can be scrubbed off.

3 Remove the filter and either replace it or clean it. Follow the manufacturer's instructions.

4 Make sure all the water is drained from the pump. If your pump is an external one, make sure the system is drained.

5 Read the manufacturer's instructions, and carry out any other servicing that is necessary before storing the pump in a dry place. It may be necessary to send it away for a service, in which case do it now instead of waiting until spring.

DISPOSE OF GARDEN WASTE . . . WISELY

Gardeners always acquire a lot of unwanted debris in the autumn, but there is no one simple way to deal with it all. Be environmentally friendly and recycle as much as possible through composting.

To improve the chances of good compost, add a layer of manure or a ready-made compost activator after every 6in of kitchen and garden refuse. Woody material such as hedge clippings and pruning will rot down too slowly to put straight on to the compost heap. These are best put through a shredder, then composted or used as a mulch. Some things are best buried or sent to the local landfill – diseased material and pernicious perennial weeds for instance, as well as woody material if you don't have a shredder. Burning at home is rarely an option.

A large quantity of leaves is better composted separately. Some leaves rot down slowly, but the end product is particularly useful for adding to potting mixtures.

TAKE HARDWOOD CUTTINGS

Hardwood cuttings root more slowly than most of the softwood or semi-ripe cuttings that you can take during the spring and summer, but they need much less attention. They don't need heat, and because you plant them in the open ground (or in a cold frame), watering won't be an onerous chore.

Many shrubs, and even trees, can be raised from hardwood cuttings. Some of them are suggested in the box below.

1 Choose stems that are firm and hard but not old and thick (pencil thickness is about right). With shrubs like this dogwood you should be able to make several cuttings from one shoot. The length of the cutting will depend on the plant, but about 6in is appropriate for most. Make a cut straight across the stem, just below a node.

2 Make the second cut about 6in above the first, and above a node, but this time at an angle so that you will know which is the top and which the bottom of the cutting.

3 Although a rooting hormone is not essential, it should increase the success rate, especially with plants that are difficult to root. Moisten the bases of the cuttings in water.

SHRUBS TO PROPAGATE

The list below is just a selection of the shrubs that usually root easily from hardwood cuttings, but there are many others. Be prepared to experiment, or consult a specialist book to see which plants are normally rooted by this method.
Aucuba japonica (spotted laurel)
Buddleia (butterfly bush)
Cornus alba (dogwood)
Cornus stolonifera (dogwood) – illustrated
Forsythia
Ligustrum ovalifolium (privet)
Philadelphus (mock orange)
Ribes sanguineum (flowering currant)

Rosa (species and hybrids)
Salix (willow)
Spiraea
Viburnum (deciduous species)

4 Dip the moistened ends into a rooting powder. You can also use liquid and gel rooting hormones, in which case you should not dip the end in water first. Treat only the base end of each cutting.

5 Make a slit trench with a spade, a little shallower than the length of the cuttings. Choose a position where the cuttings can be left undisturbed for a year.

6 Sprinkle some grit or coarse sand in the base of the slit if the ground is poorly drained. This will help to prevent water-logging around the cuttings.

7 Insert the cuttings 3–4in apart, upright against the back of the slit, leaving about 1–2in above the ground.

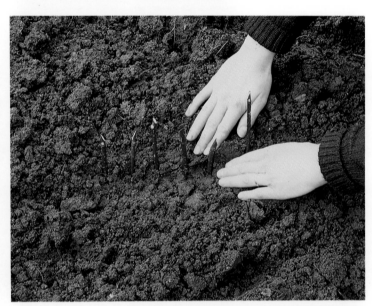

8 Firm the soil around the cuttings, to eliminate the pockets of air that would cause the cutting to dry out.

9 Water the cuttings and label. Remember to water them in dry weather.

TREES FROM HARDWOOD CUTTINGS

Some trees can also be propagated from hardwood cuttings, and those below are particularly easy.

If propagating trees, decide whether you want a multi-stemmed tree or one with a single main stem. If the latter, set the cuttings deeper in the trench so that the top bud is just below the surface of the soil.

Platanus (plane)
Populus (poplar) – illustrated
Salix (willow)

AUTUMN CLEAN THE GREENHOUSE

Autumn is an ideal time to clean the greenhouse. It is likely to be less full than in spring, and it is important to start the season of cold, dull days with clean glass to allow in all available light, and an environment as free as possible of pests and diseases.

1 If you have not already removed the remains of summer shading, do it as soon as possible. Shading washes like this are easy to wipe off with a duster if dry.

2 Whether or not summer shading has been used, clean the glass. The easiest way to clean the outside is with a brush or cleaning head on a long handle. Spray with water, adding a little detergent if necessary, and rub clean. Rinse with clean water.

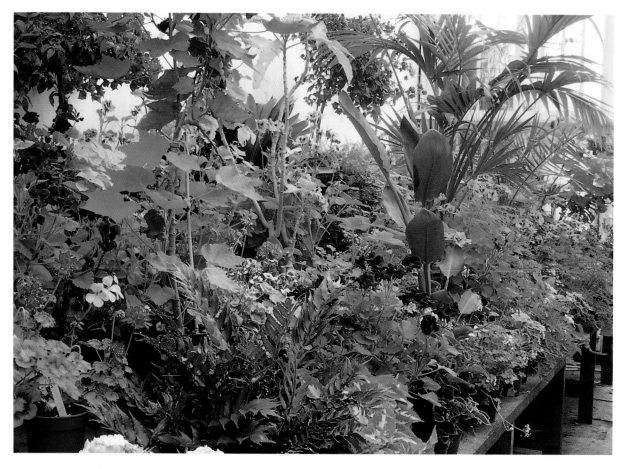

LEFT: *Even if the greenhouse is still filled with color, autumn is a good time to give the structure, shelves and benches a thorough cleaning.*

3 A ready-made glass cleaner will be very effective in removing dirt and grime, but is usually only practical for a small greenhouse where you can easily reach the glass. Clean the glass inside as well as out.

4 Algae often grow where the panes of glass overlap, an area that also traps dirt. Try squirting a jet of water between the panes, then dislodge the dirt with a thin strip of rigid plastic (a plastic plant label usually works well).

5 Finally, squirt another jet of water between the panes to move the loosened dirt and algae.

6 Dirt and soil also accumulates where the glass joins the base, and this can be a breeding ground for pests and diseases. Use a label or a small tool to lift the soil out of the crevice, then douse with a garden disinfectant (keep away from plants).

7 Fumigation is a good way to control a number of pests and diseases that may be lurking in nooks and crannies around the greenhouse. You may be able to keep some or all of the plants in, or you can fumigate an empty greenhouse. Check the label.

8 It is worth disinfecting the frame and staging, whether or not you fumigate the greenhouse. Rather than use a household disinfectant, use one sold for the garden and greenhouse.

9 Diseases are easily carried over from one plant to another on old pots and seed trays. When you have a moment between now and spring, wash them all in a garden disinfectant, scrubbing them well. The inside is as important as the outside.

WINTER

A well-planned garden will not be devoid of color or interest in the winter months, and working outdoors can be a real pleasure.
There are always jobs to be done, and tackling them now relieves the pressure in spring.
Sometimes there is no choice but to become an armchair gardener.
This is the time to scan your gardening books and plant encyclopedias for ideas, perhaps plan minor improvements or even totally redesign your garden, and of course fill in your seed order – perhaps one of the most pleasurable jobs of all.

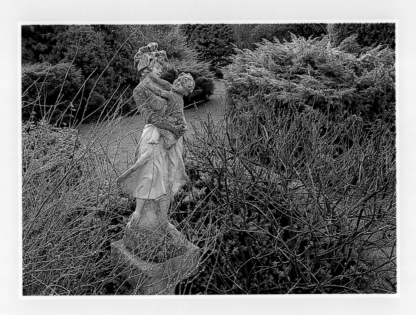

OPPOSITE: *The red-stemmed* Cornus alba *remain bright and interesting throughout the winter.*

ABOVE: *Focal points like this ornament can help to compensate for the lack of color during the cold months.*

EARLY WINTER

The ONSET OF WINTER INEVITABLY MEANS fewer jobs to do in the garden, but it is a good idea to get outdoors whenever the weather is favorable. There is always tidying-up to be done, and things like broken fences to be mended. It makes sense to get jobs like this finished before the more severe winter weather makes them less appealing. This is an especially good time to take a critical look at how you can improve your soil in time for the next growing season.

JOBS IN BRIEF

The kitchen garden

- ☐ Test your soil
- ☐ Apply lime to your soil if the test shows it is necessary
- ☐ Dig over the vegetable plot
- ☐ Prune black currants, gooseberries and raspberries
- ☐ Plant bare-root fruit bushes and trees
- ☐ Check the condition of stakes, and clean them up if necessary. Stand the ends in a wood preservative for a day if not already done so
- ☐ Finish picking late apples
- ☐ Lift leeks and parsnips as required for use. If the weather is severe, lift leeks in a mild period and heel in so that they are easy to lift when the ground is frozen
- ☐ Start forcing rhubarb

BELOW: *Warm up with some winter digging. Here the ground is being marked out.*

The flower garden

- ☐ Check bulbs, corms and tubers in store
- ☐ Get rid of garden refuse by composting
- ☐ Service your mower or have it done professionally

BELOW: *Service your mower and prepare it for winter storage.*

- ☐ Plant bare-root and balled trees and shrubs
- ☐ Check bulbs being grown in pots for early flowering
- ☐ Protect vulnerable plants that will remain in the garden
- ☐ Order seeds
- ☐ Take hardwood shrub cuttings
- ☐ Take root cuttings
- ☐ Plant hedges
- ☐ Install a pond heater if you live in a cold area where thick ice is a problem
- ☐ Remove leaves that have fallen on rock plants
- ☐ Cover alpines that need protection from winter wet with a pane of glass
- ☐ Protect flowers of winter plants that might be spoilt by the weather

The greenhouse and conservatory

- ☐ Once a week check all plants and pick off any dead or dying leaves before they start to rot
- ☐ Ventilate on warm days, especially if the greenhouse is well insulated. Lack of air movement can encourage diseases
- ☐ Except with winter-flowering plants that are still in strong, active growth, gradually give plants less water. Most will then tolerate low temperatures better and diseases should be less of a problem

BELOW: *When indoor hyacinths are over, cut off the dead flower heads.*

- ☐ Clear out the gutters, which may have become clogged with autumn leaves
- ☐ Clean the glass to make the most of the poor winter light

ABOVE: Jasminum nudiflorum, *one of the delights of winter.*

LEFT: Pyracantha *'Watereri', brilliant even in the grip of winter.*

PLANTS AT THEIR BEST

Chimonanthus praecox (shrub)
Erica carnea (shrub)
Erica × darleyensis (shrub)
Hamamelis mollis (shrub)
Iris unguicularis (syn. *I. stylosa*)
(herbaceous)
Ilex, berries (hollies)
Jasminum nudiflorum (wall shrub)
Liriope muscari (herbaceous)
Mahonia 'Charity' (shrub)
Nerine bowdenii (bulb)
Pernettya, berries (shrub)
Prunus × subhirtella 'Autumnalis'
(tree)
Pyracantha, berries (shrub)
Sarcococca (shrub)
Viburnum × bobnantense (shrub)
Viburnum farreri (syn. *V. fragrans*)
(shrub)
Viburnum tinus (shrub)

WINTER DIG THE VEGETABLE PLOT

If you have a vegetable plot, or other large area of ground that requires digging, this is a good time to do it. If the soil is a heavy clay, leaving it rough-dug over the winter will allow frost and the weather to help break down large clods. This will make it easier to rake level and to produce a seedbed of fine, crumbly soil in spring. You may prefer to leave digging a light, sandy soil until spring, as this type of soil tends to become flattened and compacted by winter rain if dug too early. New weed growth may also be a problem by spring and can be dealt with at the same time.

1 Divide the space to be dug in half lengthways, marking the area with string. Dividing the plot like this avoids moving excavated soil from one end of the plot to the other.

2 Open up a trench the depth and width of a spade blade. Pile the soil at the end of the other half of the plot, as shown.

3 When you remove the next trench, throw the soil forward into the space left by the first. Digging is easier if you first 'cut' a slice the width of the bite of soil to be dug.

4 Push the spade in parallel to the trench, taking a slice of soil about 6–8in deep. Larger bites may be too heavy to lift comfortably.

5 Loosen the soil by pulling back on the handle, while trying to keep the bite of soil on the spade.

6 Flick the soil over with the wrist, inverting the clod of earth so that the top is buried. Lift with your knees, not your back.

7 When the end of the plot is reached, fill the trench with soil taken from the first row of the return strip.

8 Finally, fill the trench left when digging has been completed with the soil put on one side from the initial excavation.

DOUBLE DIGGING

Single digging is adequate for most plants, and adding manure or garden compost in this top layer is likely to do more good for short-rooted plants like lettuces and cabbages than burying it deeply. However, for certain deep-rooted crops, such as runner beans, or to break up neglected ground, double digging can be useful. Bear in mind that it also doubles the effort!

1 Divide the plot up in the same way as described for single digging, and deal with the soil from the end of each strip in the same way. But this time make the trenches about 16in wide and 10in deep.

2 Spread a generous layer of well-rotted manure or garden compost – or other bulky organic material that will retain moisture and add humus – over the bottom of the trench.

3 Fork this thick layer of manure or organic material into the bottom of the trench. A fork is better than a spade because it will penetrate the harder lower layer more easily and will mix the material into the soil better.

4 Move the garden line to the next position, maintaining the same 16in spacing, or thereabouts. Cut and slice the soil and throw it forward as before, but take several bites per strip, otherwise the soil will be too heavy.

TEST YOUR SOIL

Many people garden successfully without ever testing their soil, but they are probably fortunate in gardening on ground that is not deficient in nutrients, is neither too acid nor too alkaline, and receives plenty of nutrients anyway as part of normal cultivation. If things don't seem to be growing well, a soil test is the best starting point for putting things right, and avid growers test their soil routinely once a year.

Professional soil testing is the most accurate for nutrients, but you can get a reasonable idea of the major nutrients in your soil with simple indicator kits. Testing for pH (see the box opposite) is quick and effective.

Bear in mind that kits vary from one manufacturer to another, so always follow the manufacturer's instructions if they vary from the advice given here.

1 Collect the soil sample from about 2–3in below the surface. This gives a more typical reading of nutrient levels in the root area. Take a number of samples from around the garden, but test each one separately.

2 With this kit one part of soil is mixed with five parts of water. Shake together vigorously in a clean jar, then allow the water to settle. This can take between half an hour and a day, depending on the soil.

3 Draw off some settled liquid from the top inch or so for your test.

4 Carefully transfer the solution to the test and reference chambers in the plastic container, using the pipette provided.

5 Select the appropriate color-coded capsule (different ones are used for each major nutrient) and empty the powder it contains into the test chamber. Replace the cap, then shake vigorously.

6 After a few minutes, compare the color of the liquid with the shade panel that forms part of the container. The kit contains an explanation of the significance of each reading, and what – if anything – to do.

WHAT IS pH?

The term pH is a scientific way of stating how acid or alkaline something is. Soils vary in their degree of acidity or alkalinity. The scale runs from 0 (most acid) to 14 (most alkaline), with 7 as neutral. Soils never reach these extremes, and horticulturally, 6.5 can be considered neutral in that it is the pH at which most plants will grow happily. Acid-loving plants, such as rhododendrons, camellias, peonies (see above) and heathers, need a lower pH and may develop chlorosis – a yellowing of the leaves – if grown on alkaline soil. Alkaline-loving plants like lilacs prefer a pH of 7 or above.

These differences may sound small, but on the pH scale 1 point represents a ten-fold increase in acidity or alkalinity.

TESTING THE pH

Collect your samples and mix with water as described for nutrient testing, but for the pH test you don't have to wait for the mixture to settle, and only the test chamber is filled with the solution. Clean water is used for the reference chamber. Add the indicator chemical provided with the kit, then put the top on and shake vigorously. Compare the color with the shade panel on the container for the nearest pH value.

USING PROBE METERS

Probes that measure the pH on a dial are very quick and easy to use, but some people consider them less accurate than color indicator tests. To ensure an accurate reading, follow the instructions and keep the tip clean.

Push the probe into the soil, and take the reading once the needle seems to have settled. Take several readings from the same area to check results, then move on to another part of the garden.

ADDING LIME TO THE SOIL

Never add lime unless you have tested your soil first and know that it is necessary. Too much lime applied regularly can be harmful for your plants. Always check that you are applying the right sort of lime at the appropriate application rate. Your testing kit should contain advice about how much lime (which will vary with type) to apply to your soil to adjust the pH.

1 Hydrated lime, often used for gardens, should not be handled unnecessarily. Always use gloves, and goggles to protect your eyes. Ground limestone is safer to handle.

2 Rake the lime into the surface, whichever kind of lime you use.

PROTECT WINTER HELLEBORE FLOWERS

Winter-flowering hellebores such as *Helleborus niger* (Christmas rose) are frost-hardy, but their pale blooms are often only just above soil level.

If you want to cut the flowers to take indoors, covering the plants will reduce mud splashes and keep the blooms clean and in good condition.

1 Protect low-growing winter-flowering plants such as *H. niger* with a cloche if you want perfect blooms to cut for indoors. Though frost-hardy, the flowers tend to become splashed with mud and damaged by the weather.

2 If you don't have a cloche, improvise with a piece of polyethlyene over wire hoops, or a pane of glass supported on bricks.

ABOVE RIGHT: Helleborus argutifolius *is a tall species that will not need protection.*

RIGHT: Helleborus orientalis *may benefit from protection for early cut blooms.*

CHECK BULBS AND CORMS IN STORE

Don't wait until it is time to plant your tender overwintering bulbs before checking them for

rot. Storage rots are common, and easily spread from affected bulbs or corms to healthy ones.

1 Bulbs, corms and tubers being over-wintered in a frost-free place should be checked once a month. By eliminating diseased or soft bulbs or corms, you will prevent the rot spreading to others.

2 If you discover soft or diseased bulbs in store, it's worth dusting the others with a fungicide. Check with the label to ensure that it is suitable for the purpose, and be careful not to inhale the dust.

SERVICING YOUR MOWER

Winter is the best time to have your mower serviced. The chances are you won't bother once it is in regular use during the summer. You may prefer to have the servicing done professionally, which is often cheaper at this time than in spring, but you can do some of the simple tasks yourself. The advice below should be followed in conjunction with your handbook.

1 Remove accumulated clippings and dirt from around the blade housing of a rotary mower, being certain that any power supply is disconnected. Use an abrasive paper to clean metal blades.

2 Wipe the blade with an oily rag or spray with an anti-rust aerosol. If the blade is in poor condition, replace it with a new one. On appropriate models you may consider replacing it with a plastic blade for safety.

3 If you have a gasoline mower, drain the fuel and oil before storing the machine for the winter.

4 Remove the spark plug, clean it and reset the gap if necessary. If the plug is in poor condition, replace with a new one.

5 Pour a tablespoonful of oil into the cylinder and pull the starter to turn the engine over half a dozen times before you return the spark plug, thus coating the engine.

6 Brush or wipe away accumulated clippings from a cylinder mower. If the mower is electric, disconnect the power supply before you start.

7 Wipe the mower with an oily rag, or spray with an anti-rust aerosol, before you store it.

8 Oil the chain if your mower is fitted with one. You may have to remove the chain guard to reach it.

BRING ON FORCED BULBS

Whether your bulbs flower at Christmas, or on any particular date, depends partly on whether you used prepared bulbs in the first place. However, timing also depends on how cold you have kept the bulbs and at what point you bring them out from their resting place into light and warmth.

1 Check bowls of bulbs plunged outdoors beneath sand, peat or grit used to keep them cool and dark while roots develop. If the shoots are about 1in high, it is time to bring them indoors.

2 If you have kept bulbs in a cool, dark place indoors, in a cupboard or loft, check these periodically too. Bring them into the light when the shoots are 1–2in tall.

ABOVE: *Moss provides a more instant way of improving the appearance of a bowl or basket of bulbs. Lift clumps of moss, with roots intact, from your garden and cover the surface.*

3 Wipe the container clean if it has been plunged outdoors, then place in a light but cool position indoors or in a conservatory. Only put in a warm place once the buds have emerged and are beginning to show color, else the stems may be too long and weak.

4 If you sow grass seed on the surface as soon as you bring the bulbs into the light, you should have an attractive carpet of grass by the time they flower.

5 Just before the bulbs come into full flower, cut the grass to a height of about 1–2in, to make it look even and neat.

WHEN FLOWERING IS OVER

Never attempt to grow the same bulbs indoors for a second year, with the exception of indoor plants like amaryllis (*Hippeastrum*) – see the box below for more information. Forcing hardy bulbs to flower indoors drains their reserves and results are almost always disappointing a second time. But there is no need to discard them. Plant them in the garden where they should gradually recover over a few seasons.

1 If you plan to keep your bulbs to grow in the garden, dead-head them as soon as the display is over. This will avoid energy being wasted on seed production.

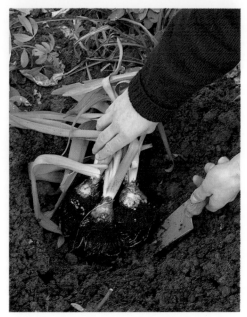

3 In spring, plant the bulbs out in a border or other spot where they can be left undisturbed to grow as a natural group. Some types of bulb may not produce flowers the following season, but probably will do so in subsequent years.

KEEPING AMARYLLIS TO FLOWER AGAIN

The houseplant popularly known as amaryllis is really a *Hippeastrum*. Many are sold in flower during the winter, or as bulbs that grow with phenomenal speed once started. You should be able to keep them so that they flower another year if you follow this advice.

● Cut the flower stalks close to their point of origin once the flowers fade.

● Keep watered, and feed occasionally.

● From late spring onwards keep in a greenhouse or conservatory if possible.

● If you don't have a greenhouse or conservatory, stand the plant outside for the summer.

● Let the foliage die down in late summer or the autumn.

● Start into growth again in late autumn or early winter.

2 Do not plant directly into the garden, but acclimatize them gradually by placing in a cold frame or other cool but protected place. Regular watering and a dose of liquid feed will help them recover.

ABOVE: *Amaryllis should flower the following year – the box, left, tells you how.*

MID WINTER

IF YOU MADE AN EARLY START with winter jobs like digging and tidying beds and borders, mid winter is a time mainly for indoor jobs like ordering seeds and plants, writing labels, and designing improvements for the year ahead.

These are not unimportant tasks, and by attending to them in good time you are more likely to make the right decisions and have everything ready for late winter and early spring when gardening begins again in earnest.

JOBS IN BRIEF

The kitchen garden

- ☐ Test your soil
- ☐ Apply lime if your soil needs it
- ☐ Continue winter digging
- ☐ Force rhubarb
- ☐ Sow fava beans under cloches in mild areas

BELOW: *Winter is a good time to test your soil, and kits like this make it easy.*

BELOW: *This is the time to start thinking about forcing rhubarb.*

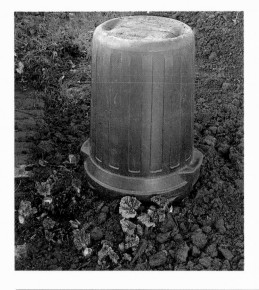

The flower garden

- ☐ Check bulbs, corms and tubers in store
- ☐ Service your mower or have it done professionally
- ☐ Check bulbs being grown in pots for early flowering
- ☐ Order seeds, bulbs and plants for the coming season
- ☐ Take hardwood shrub cuttings
- ☐ Take root cuttings
- ☐ Keep an area of water open in an iced over pond if there is a prolonged freeze. If you don't have a pond heater, try standing a pan of boiling water on the ice until it melts through
- ☐ Protect flowers of winter plants that might be spoilt by the weather
- ☐ Knock heavy snow off hedges and conifers if the branches start to bend under the weight. If you leave it, the shape may be spoilt
- ☐ Insulate the cold frame for extra protection against the coldest weather

BELOW: *Fish will appreciate it if you melt a hole in the ice during a prolonged freeze.*

The greenhouse and conservatory

- ☐ Once a week check all plants and pick off any dead or dying leaves before they start to rot
- ☐ Ventilate on warm days
- ☐ Start off overwintered chrysanthemum stools (roots) to provide cuttings
- ☐ Start sowing seeds if you can provide sufficient warmth to germinate them and a very light position in which to grow the seedlings afterwards

BELOW: *Chrysanthemum cuttings are easy to root, and now is a good time to take them.*

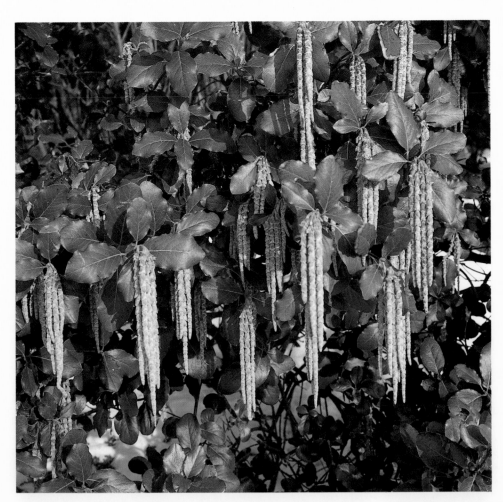

PLANTS AT THEIR BEST

Chimonanthus praecox (shrub)
Eranthis hyemalis (bulb)
Erica carnea (shrub)
Erica × darleyensis (shrub)
Galanthus nivalis (bulb)
Garrya elliptica (shrub)
Hamamelis mollis (shrub)
Iris unguicularis (syn. *I. stylosa*)
(herbaceous)
Ilex, berries (hollies)
Jasminum nudiflorum (wall shrub)
Lonicera fragrantissima (shrub)
Prunus × subhirtella 'Autumnalis'
(tree)
Sarcococca (shrub)
Viburnum × bodnantense (shrub)
Viburnum farreri (syn. *V. fragrans*)
(shrub)
Viburnum tinus (shrub)

LEFT: Garrya elliptica.

BELOW LEFT: Viburnum *x* bodnantense
'Dawn', in bloom in mid winter.

BELOW: Hamamelis mollis.

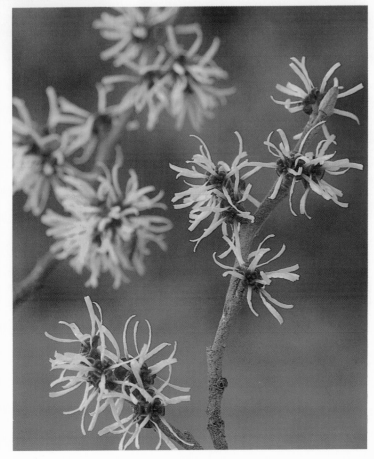

FORCE RHUBARB

Rhubarb is one of those crops that almost looks after itself, and if you have an established clump, forcing tender young stems is very easy. There are many methods of forcing rhubarb, and they all seem to work well. Just choose a technique that you find convenient.

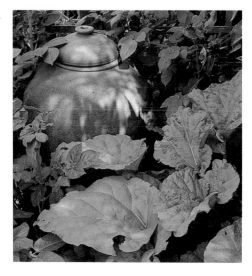

ABOVE: *Rhubarb is a useful early crop that you can start forcing now. A terracotta forcing pot is shown in the background.*

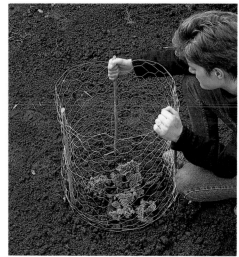

1 Choose a method of excluding light. Special pots were once used for this, but now most people improvise. An old tea chest, bucket, or barrel are simple but effective alternatives. If you don't have these, make a frame from wire-netting and stakes as shown here.

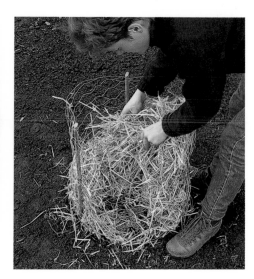

2 Pile straw into the wire-netting cage, pressing it well down, to provide warmth and protection.

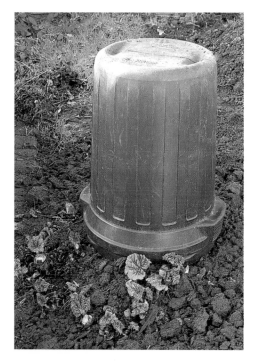

3 Another simple way to make a rhubarb forcer is with a plastic trash can. If you don't mind cutting the bottom out of it, use it the right way up with a lid on, otherwise use it inverted without a lid.

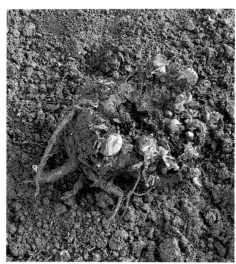

4 For really early crops many gardeners lift a well-established root to leave on the surface for a few weeks. This gives the root a cold spell that makes it think winter is more advanced than it is.

5 Replant your chilled crown for outdoor forcing, or bring it into the greenhouse. If you have a warm greenhouse, place it under the bench, screened with black plastic. Alternatively, pot it up and put in a plastic bag to take indoors. Make sure there is plenty of air in the bag by keeping it loose and making a few small air holes, then place the bag in a warm yet convenient place – under the stairs or in a kitchen cupboard. Check progress periodically.

FORCE CHICORY

Chicons, the forced and blanched new shoots produced from chicory roots, are an enjoyable winter vegetable when fresh produce is scarce.

It is best if you grow your own roots from plants sown in late spring or early summer, but you may be able to buy roots for forcing.

1 To produce chicons, you should choose a variety of chicory recommended for the purpose – 'Witloof' is an old and traditional variety. Lift the root from mid autumn onwards, and leave on the surface for a few days.

2 When the roots have been exposed for a few days, which helps to retard growth, trim the tops off to leave a 1–2in stump of growth. You can pot them up now or store them in a box of sand, peat or dry soil for use later.

WRITING LABELS IN ADVANCE

3 To force, place three roots in a 9in pot, using a moist potting soil or ordinary garden soil. You may have to trim the ends of the roots to fit them in the pot. Leave the crowns exposed.

Cover the pot with a second pot with the drainage holes blocked (use a piece of kitchen foil for this), and keep in a temperature of 50–65°F. Keep the soil mix just moist. The chicons will be ready in about three weeks time.

It makes sense to do as many jobs as you can in winter that will save time later when you are busy sowing and planting. Instead of waiting, write your labels on a day when you can't get into the garden. You will probably make a neater job of it by doing it more leisurely, and it will take pressure off the time when you're busy in the garden.

TAKE ROOT CUTTINGS

Nearly everyone takes stem cuttings at some time, but surprisingly few gardeners bother with root cuttings. Some useful plants can be propagated this way (see the box opposite for examples), and it is an interesting and relatively simple winter job, because root cuttings are only likely to be successful if taken during the dormant season.

1 Lift a young but well-established plant to provide the cuttings. If you don't want to use the whole plant for cuttings, and prefer to leave the parent plant largely undisturbed, just remove soil from one side to gain access to the roots.

2 If the plant has large, fleshy roots, cut some off close to the main stem or root. You should be able to make several cuttings from one root by cutting it into sections later.

3 Cut each root into lengths about 2in long. To help you remember which way up they are, cut them horizontally at the top and diagonally at the bottom.

4 Fill a pot with a gritty potting mixture and insert the cuttings using a dibber or pencil to make the hole. The top of the cutting should be flush with the top of the potting soil.

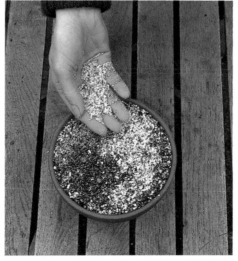

5 Sprinkle a thin layer of grit over the surface. Label, as nothing will be visible for a few months, and it's easy to forget what the pot contains. Place in a cold frame or greenhouse and keep the potting soil just moist.

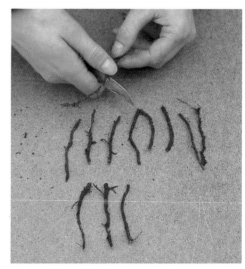

6 Some plants, such as border phlox and rock plants like *Primula denticulata*, have thin roots. These can be laid horizontally, so don't make sloping cuts to indicate the bottom. Just cut into 1–2in lengths.

7 Fill a seed tray with a gritty potting mix and firm it level.

8 Space the cuttings out evenly over the surface, then cover them with a layer of the gritty potting mix. Keep moist but not too wet, in a cold frame or greenhouse.

SOME PLANTS TO GROW FROM ROOT CUTTINGS

Acanthus
Echinops
Gaillardia
Phlox (border)
Primula denticulata
Pulsatilla vulgaris
Romneya coulteri

LEFT: *Border phlox can be propagated from root cuttings. This one is* Phlox paniculata *'Flamingo'.*

INSULATE COLD FRAMES

Old-fashioned cold frames with brick or timber sides were not as light as modern aluminum and glass or plastic cold frames, but they were warmer. Glass sides let in more light, but also lose heat rapidly. Have the best of both worlds by insulating your glass-sided cold frame during the coldest weather, while taking full advantage of the glass sides in spring and summer.

1 Sometimes there are small gaps between the glass and an aluminum frame. This does not matter in hot weather, but for winter warmth it's worth sealing the gaps with draught-proofing strip sold for windows and doors.

2 Insulate the glass sides with sheets of expanded polystyrene. Cut it with a knife or saw. Measure accurately, allowing for the thickness of the material where sheets join at the ends. Push sheets into place so that they fit tightly.

COVERING COLD FRAMES

Cold frames of any kind benefit from a warm blanket thrown over them on very cold nights. A piece of old carpet is an ideal alternative (see above). Put it in place *before* the temperature drops, and remember to remove it the next morning unless it remains exceptionally cold. Your plants need light and warmth.

TAKE CHRYSANTHEMUM CUTTINGS

Chrysanthemums that are overwintered in a greenhouse or cold frame are usually propagated from cuttings once the old stool (clump of roots) starts to produce shoots. It is better to raise vigorous young plants from cuttings than simply to replant the old clump. Chrysanthemums that have been boxed or potted up in the autumn, and kept frost-free and just moist, will soon start producing new shoots. Stimulate growth now with plenty of light and warmth.

1 When your boxes or pots of chrysanthemum stools have produced shoots about 2in long, it is time to take cuttings.

2 If possible, choose shoots coming directly from the base of the plant. Cut them off close to the base.

3 Pull off the lowest leaves and trim the ends of the cuttings straight across with a sharp knife.

4 Dip the ends in a rooting hormone. If using a powder, dip the end in water first so that it adheres. Hormone treatment usually improves the rate and speed of rooting.

5 Insert the cuttings around the edge of a pot containing a mixture suitable for cuttings.

6 If you don't have a propagator, cover the pot with a plastic bag, but inflate it to ensure it is not in contact with the leaves. Turn the bag regularly to avoid condensation dripping onto the leaves. Remove when the plants have rooted.

RIGHT: *Many chrysanthemums can make colorful garden plants for the autumn, and they are easily propagated from cuttings taken at this time of year.*

SOW SEEDS FOR SUMMER FLOWERS

It is too early to sow seeds outdoors, and it is likely to be too soon to sow most tender bedding plants in the greenhouse or on a windowsill. But it is not too soon to sow summer flowers that need a long growing period before they flower, such as fibrous rooted begonias (*Begonia semperflorens*). If in doubt, check the seed packet to see whether a particular flower needs early sowing or not.

Because it is difficult to provide the necessary warmth economically at this time of year, especially in a greenhouse, it is best to start the seeds off in a propagator, and move them out once they have germinated. By sowing in pots you will be able to germinate more kinds of seeds in your propagator at the same time. Sowing in pots is also sensible for seeds where only a few plants are needed, such as for trees and shrubs.

1 Fill the pot with a seed sowing mixture, and gently firm and level it. Using the base or top of a jar is a convenient way of doing this.

2 Sow thinly, and as evenly as possible. Bear in mind that you have to handle the seedlings later, and very close spacing will make this difficult. Most can be sprinkled easily between finger and thumb, like salt.

3 Large seeds are best spaced individually. If they are very large, you can insert them into small holes made with a dibber.

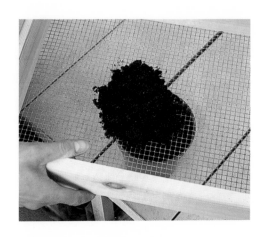

4 Most seeds should be covered with a light sprinkling of the same soil mix. Use a sieve to spread the soil evenly. Some seeds germinate best in light and should not be covered – check the sowing instructions.

5 To avoid disturbing the evenly distributed seeds, water the pot initially by standing it in shallow water. Remove the pot and let it drain when the surface looks moist.

6 If you don't have a propagator, cover the pot with a sheet of glass or plastic until the seeds germinate. Turn the covering periodically if condensation is heavy. Don't forget the label!

LATE WINTER

IN FAVORABLE AREAS LATE WINTER CAN be almost spring-like, especially in a mild winter, but don't be lulled into sowing and planting outdoors too soon. If the weather turns very cold, seeds won't germinate, and seedlings and plants may receive such a check to growth that they do not do as well as those sown or planted later.

Concentrate your efforts on indoor sowing, but make the most of frames and cloches, too, for early crops.

JOBS IN BRIEF

The kitchen garden

- ☐ Finish winter digging
- ☐ Apply manures and fertilizers where appropriate
- ☐ Force rhubarb
- ☐ Sow fava beans under cloches
- ☐ Plant shallots
- ☐ Place cloches in position to warm up the soil
- ☐ Sow early crops in cold frames or beneath cloches
- ☐ Prepare runner bean and celery trenches
- ☐ Chit 'seed' potatoes (small tubers) of early varieties
- ☐ Plant new fruit trees

BELOW: *Mulching fruit bushes now will give them a good start for the season.*

- ☐ Mulch established fruit trees and bushes with garden compost or rotted manure
- ☐ Put cloches over strawberries if you want an early crop
- ☐ Spray peaches and nectarines with a fungicide recommended for peach leaf curl if this disease is a problem where you live

The flower garden

- ☐ Plant climbers
- ☐ Check bulbs, corms and tubers in store
- ☐ Feed and mulch beds and borders
- ☐ Service your mower or have it done professionally
- ☐ Order seeds, bulbs and plants for the coming season
- ☐ Keep an area of water open in an iced-over pond if there is a prolonged freeze
- ☐ Insulate the cold frame for extra protection against the coldest weather
- ☐ Sow sweet peas
- ☐ Pinch out growing tips of autumn-sown sweet peas
- ☐ Tidy up the rock garden, and apply fresh stone chippings where necessary

BELOW: *Take time now to tidy up the rock garden.*

- ☐ Check labels on shrubs and border plants and renew if necessary
- ☐ Lay a new lawn from turf, provided the ground is not frozen

The Greenhouse and conservatory

- ☐ Take chrysanthemum cuttings
- ☐ Pot up chrysanthemums rooted earlier
- ☐ Take dahlia cuttings
- ☐ Sow seeds of bedding plants and pot-plants
- ☐ Prick out seedlings sown earlier
- ☐ Increase ventilation on warm days
- ☐ Make sure glass is clean so that the plants receive plenty of light

BELOW: *Many summer bedding plants can be sown now.*

BELOW: *Many summer bedding plants sown earlier will be ready to prick out.*

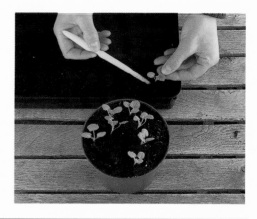

PLANTS AT THEIR BEST

Crocus (bulb)
Daphne mezereum (shrub)
Eranthis hyemalis (bulb)
Erica carnea (shrub)
Erica × darleyensis (shrub)
Galanthus nivalis (bulb)
Garrya elliptica (shrub)
Helleborus niger (herbaceous)
Helleborus orientalis (herbaceous)
Iris unguicularis (syn. *I. stylosa*)
(herbaceous)
Iris reticulata (bulb)
Jasminum nudiflorum (wall shrub)
Muscari armeniacum (bulb)
Prunus cerasifera (tree)
Prunus × subhirtella 'Autumnalis'
(tree)
Sarcococca (shrub)
Viburnum × bodnantense (shrub)
Viburnum tinus (shrub)

RIGHT: *Varieties of* Erica carnea *flower in winter and often into spring.*

BELOW: *In mild areas,* Muscari armeniacum *will put in an appearance at the end of winter.*

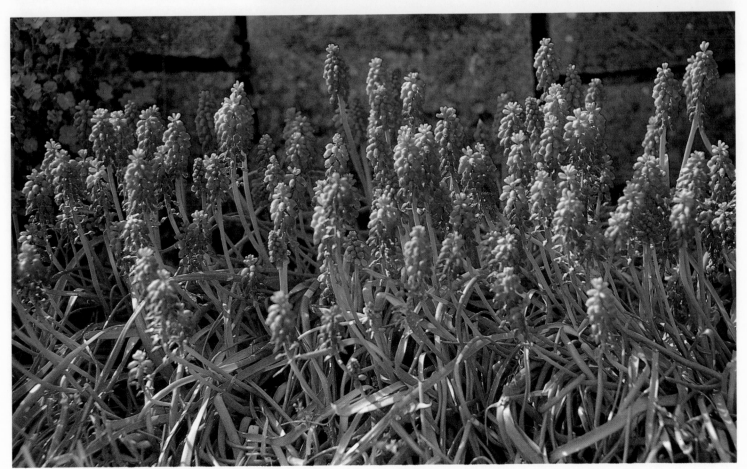

SOW EARLY CROPS IN YOUR COLD FRAME

If your cold frame is not packed with over-wintering plants, make use of it for early vegetable crops. Radishes and turnips are among the crops that grow quickly and mature early in a cold frame, but you can also try forcing varieties of carrot. Suitable varieties of lettuce also do well.

1 Dig over the ground in the frame, working in as much organic material as possible. Farmyard manure is useful for enriching the soil for these early crops. Do not apply powerful artificial fertilizers at this time.

2 Rake the soil level, and make shallow drills with the rake or a hoe. You can sow the seeds broadcast (scattered randomly), but this makes weeding and thinning more difficult.

3 Sow the seeds thinly, then rake the soil back over the drills. Water thoroughly, then keep the frame closed until the seeds germinate. Once they are through, ventilate on mild days, but keep closed, and if possible insulated, at night.

WARM UP THE SOIL

If you have a kitchen garden, start warming up the soil with cloches to get your vegetables off to an early start. Although most early vegetables are not sown until early spring, you need to have your cloches in position several weeks before you plan to sow.

1 Cloche designs vary considerably, but most can easily be made into long runs the length of the row. Make sure that they are butted close together and that plastic cloches are well anchored to the ground.

2 End pieces are essential, otherwise the cloches will just become a wind tunnel. Make sure they are fixed firmly in place.

3 Polyethylene tunnel cloches are inexpensive to buy, and although they need to be re-covered after a few seasons, a replacement sheet is inexpensive. Fix the hoops first, then stretch the sheet over them.

4 Use the special fixing wires to hold the sheet in position.

5 Secure the ends with sticks or pegs, pulling the plastic taut.

6 Heap a little soil over the edges to anchor the cloches.

PREPARE BEAN AND CELERY TRENCHES

You can grow a satisfactory crop of beans without special soil preparation, and achieve a respectable crop of self-blanching celery by planting on ground that has not been specially enriched. But if you want an especially heavy and impressive crop, it is worth preparing the trench.

1 Open up a trench about 10–12in deep and 2ft wide for runner beans, 15in wide for celery. Heap the soil to one or both sides of the trench.

2 Add as much rotted manure or garden compost as you can spare. This will add some nutrients and benefit the structure and moisture-holding capacity of the soil.

3 Fork the manure or garden compost into the soil at the bottom of the trench – don't leave it as a layer. Finally, rake the soil back into the trench.

APPLY SLOW-ACTING FERTILIZERS

Apply slow-acting fertilizers such as bonemeal and ready-made controlled-release fertilizers when the vegetable plot has been dug and levelled, ready for sowing from early spring onwards. Controlled-release fertilizers release their nutrients only when the soil is warm enough for the plants to use them. Fertilizers should always be applied evenly and at the recommended rate.

1 Divide the area into yard-wide strips with string, and space stakes at the same interval to form a square. Scatter the measured dose, then move the stakes. Rake into the soil.

TAKE DAHLIA CUTTINGS

If you require just one or two more dahlia plants, you can simply divide the tubers before planting them in late spring, making sure that each piece has an 'eye' or bud. For more plants, it is best to take cuttings after starting the tubers into growth early in the greenhouse.

1 Plant the tubers in deep boxes of soil mix. You will not be able to bury the tubers, but that does not matter so long as you trickle as much soil as possible around them. Keep the boxes in a light, warm place.

2 Take the cuttings when they have two or three pairs of leaves. If you take a tiny piece of the parent tuber, they should root quickly without a rooting hormone.

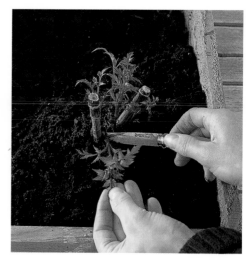

3 You can take larger cuttings if you miss the earlier stage, but try not to let them become longer than 3in. Cut off with a sharp knife just above the tuber.

4 Remove the lowest pair of leaves to leave a clear stem. Pull the leaves off carefully or cut them off with a sharp knife. If some of the leaves have grown large, cut these in half and discard the tips. This will reduce the area of leaf through which moisture can be lost while the cutting is rooting.

5 To increase the number of cuttings likely to root successfully, dip the cut ends into a rooting hormone. Insert the cuttings around the edge of a pot, label, then place in a propagator to root.

6 If you don't have a propagator, enclose the pot and cuttings in a plastic bag. Try to keep the leaves out of contact with the bag. They should root in a matter of weeks if you keep them in a warm, light position.

PLANT CLIMBERS

You can plant container-grown climbers at almost any time of the year provided the ground is not frozen or waterlogged. However, it is much easier to train in new shoots as they grow than it is to untangle them from their temporary support and attempt to retrain them.

1 Excavate a hole about twice the diameter of the root-ball. The center of the plant should be at least 12in away from the wall or fence, otherwise the roots will be too dry.

2 Dig in a generous amount of rotted manure or garden compost. This is particularly important when planting a climber near a wall or fence, as you need material that will hold moisture around the roots.

3 Tease out some of the fine roots from around the edge of the rootball, to encourage the plant to root out into the surrounding soil. Return and firm the soil around the plant, and apply a slow or controlled-release fertilizer.

4 Loosen the stems first if they have been tied to a stake, then tie them to the support. Spread them out evenly, and don't be afraid to spread them wide and low – new shoots will grow upwards to fill the space.

5 Water thoroughly after planting, and be prepared to water regularly in dry weather for the first year. Climbers are usually planted where walls or other plants shield them from most of the rain.

6 Apply a mulch at least 2in thick around the plant after the ground has been soaked thoroughly. This will reduce water loss as well as suppress weeds.

SOW BEDDING PLANTS

Late winter is a good time to sow the majority of frost-tender plants used for summer bedding if you have a heated greenhouse, although a few such as pelargonium (bedding geraniums) and *Begonia semperflorens* are best sown earlier to give them a long period of growth before planting out in late spring or early summer. Quick-growers, such as alyssum and French marigolds (*Tagetes patula*), will soon catch up even if you sow in early or mid spring.

Because you usually need quite a lot of each kind for bedding, it is normally best to sow the seeds in trays rather than pots. However, you may prefer to use pots for the more difficult seeds that need to be germinated in a propagator, as you can pack more in.

1 Fill a seed tray with a sterilized soil mix suitable for seeds and seedlings. A potting mix could inhibit germination or harm some seedlings. Strike the soil mix off level with the rim of the tray.

2 Use a presser board (a scrap of wood cut to the right size will usually do the job) and press the compost gently until it is firmed about ½in below the rim.

3 Water the tray now, before you sow. This should provide enough moisture for the seeds initially, and won't wash fine seeds away or to one side of the tray.

4 Very large seeds can be spaced by hand, but most medium-sized seeds are easily scattered with a folded piece of stiff paper. Tap it with a finger as you move it over the surface.

5 Unless the packet advises not to cover the seeds (a few germinate better if exposed to light), cover them by sifting more of the sowing mixture over the top.

6 Unless you are placing the tray in a propagator, cover it with a sheet of glass, or place it in a plastic bag. Turn the glass over or the bag inside out regularly (it may be necessary to do this every day) to prevent condensation drips.

7 Remove any covering when the first seeds start to germinate. If you don't, the seedlings may succumb to diseases. It may be possible to reduce the amount of warmth needed once the seeds have germinated, but good light is essential.

SOWING FINE SEEDS

Very tiny seeds, like lobelia and begonia, are difficult to handle and to spread evenly. Mix them with a small quantity of silver sand to provide greater bulk, then sprinkle the sand and seed mix between finger and thumb as you move your hand over the surface of the tray.

PRICK OUT BEDDING PLANTS

Seeds sown in mid winter may be ready for pricking out, and even those sown in late winter may be ready to move on soon. Never let seedlings become overcrowded after germination.

1 Fill seed trays with a potting mixture recommended for seedlings. Strike the soil mix off level, then firm it with fingers or a pressing board.

2 Prick out a seedling by loosening the soil and lifting up the plant by its seed leaves (the first ones that open, which usually look very different from the true leaves).

3 Make a hole in the potting mix, deep enough to take most of the roots without curling them. Gently firm the soil mix around the roots.

4 To help produce an evenly spaced box of plants, first prick out a row along the end and one side. When you have this spacing right, fill in the rest of the tray.

5 Exact spacing will depend on the type of plant you are pricking out. Large ones need more space than small ones. You are unlikely to fit more than 40 plants in a seed tray.

6 If you find it more convenient, use a modular tray system. This makes spacing easier, and there is less root disturbance when the plants are put in the garden later.

SUPPLIERS

The following names and addresses are useful first contacts for many of the plants and gardening accessories that you may need to buy. In the space available, however, we can give only a small selection, and in most cases there are many more excellent suppliers that could be mentioned. Don't forget that the best place to start is often your local garden centre. Often they can obtain items not in stock, or may be able to suggest a suitable supplier.

GARDEN EQUIPMENT AND SUPPLIES

Agway, Inc.
P.O. Box 4746
Syracuse, NY 13221
Tel: (315) 449-7620
Nationwide franchise farm and garden supplies; call for nearest location

Gardens Alive
5100 Schenley Place
Lawrenceburg, IN 47025
Tel: (812) 537-8650
Organic garden supplies – free catalog available

Gardener's Supply Company
128 Intervale Road
Burlington, VT 05401
Tel: (800) 688-5510
Free catalog available

Kinsman Company
River Road
Point Pleasant, PA 18950
1-800-733-5613
Free catalog available

Smith & Hawkin
25 Corte Madera
Mill Valley, CA 94941
Tel: (415) 383-2000
Clothing, tools, as well as garden furniture and ornaments – free catalog available

NURSERIES

Brecks
US Reservation Center
6523 North Galena Rd.
Peoria, IL 61632
Tel: (309) 691-4616
Bulbs – catalog available

Burpee Gardens
300 Park Avenue
Warminster, PA 18991–0001
Tel: (215) 674-9633
Seeds and plants, trees, shrubs and vines – catalog available

Camellia Forest Nursery
125 Carolina Forest Road
Chapel Hill, NC 27516
Tel: (919) 967-5529
Camellia and camellia seeds of all varieties, oriental trees – catalog available

Canyon Creek Nursery
3527 Dry Creek Road
Oroville, CA 95965
Tel: (916) 533-2166
Plants, perennials, unusual and rare, especially salvias – catalog available

Foliage Gardens
2003 128th Avenue, SE
Bellevue, WA 98005
Tel: (206) 747-2998
Wide variety of ferns – catalog available

Fox Hill Farm
Box 7
Parma, MI 49269
Tel: (517) 531-3179
Herbs, perennials – catalog available

The Fragrant Path
P.Q. Box 328
Fort Calhoun, NE 68023
Seeds, annuals, perennials, herbs, trees, and shrubs – fragrance emphasized – catalog available

Grigsby Cactus Gardens
2326 Bella Vista Drive
Vista, CA 92084
Tel: (619) 727-1323
Cacti, succulents – catalog available

Hastings, H.G., Co.
Box 4274
Atlanta, GA 30302
Tel: (800) 334-1771
Southeast garden specialists – catalog available

Jackson & Perkins
P.O. Box 1028
Medford, OR 97501
Tel: (800) 292-4769
Perennials, wide variety of roses – catalog available

Klehm Nursery
Rt. 5, 197 Penny Road
South Barrington, IL 60010
Tel: (312) 551-3715
Plants, peonies, daylilies – catalog available

Logee's Greenhouses
141 North Street
Danielson, CT 06239
Tel: (203) 774-8038
Plants, including large selection of rarities, tropicals, and orchids – catalog available

Milaeger's Gardens
4838 Douglas Avenue
Racine, WI 53402–2371
Tel: (414) 639-2371
Catalog available

Musser Forests, Inc.
P.O. Box 340
Indiana, PA 15701–0340
Tel: (412) 465-5685
Seedlings, trees, and shrubs – catalog available

Paradise Water Gardens
672 May Street
Whitman, MA 02382
Tel: (716) 447-4711
Lilies, bog plants, etc., supplies, books – catalog available

Plants of the Southwest
930 Baca Street
Sante Fe, NM 87501
Tel: (505) 471-2212
Drought-tolerant plants – catalog available

Shady Oaks Nursery
700 19th Avenue, NE
Waseca, MN 56093
Tel: (507) 835-5055
Plants, ferns, wildflowers and shrubs, hostas, shade-tolerant perennials – catalog available

Shepherds Garden Seeds
30 Irene Street
Torrington, CT 06790
Tel: (203) 482-3638
Seeds, vegetables, herbs, annuals, many vintage and unusual

Stark Bro's Nurseries & Orchards Co.
P.O. Box 10
Louisiana, NO 63353–0010
Tel: (800) 325-4180
Fruit trees, berries, trees, shrubs, and ground cover – catalog available

Thompson & Morgan
P.O. Box 1308
Jackson, NJ 08527–0308
Tel: (201) 363-2225
Seeds, huge list of perennials, vegetables, and annuals – free catalog available

Van Ness Water Gardens
2460 North Euclid
Upland, CA 91786–1199
Tel: (714) 982-2425
*Water and bog plants, supplies –
catalog available*

Wayside Gardens
1 Garden Lane
Hodges, SC 29695–0001
Tel: (800) 845-1124
*Plants, landscape and fruit trees,
and flowering shrubs – catalog
available*

Well-Sweep Herb Farm
317 Mt. Bethel Road
Port Murray, NJ 07865
Tel: (908) 852-5390
*Perennials and herbs – catalog
available*

WATER GARDEN SUPPLIERS

Discount Pond Supplies
P.O. Box 423371 H
Kissimmee, FL 34742–3371
Fax: (407) 932-4019
*Complete line of water garden
supplies – free catalog available*

Patio Garden Ponds
P.O. Box 890402
Oklahoma City, OK 73189–
0402
*Rubber pond liners, pumps, and
filters – catalog available*

**Resource Conservation
Technology, Inc.**
2633 North Calvert Street
Baltimore, MD 21218
Tel: (410) 366-1146
Rubber liners for garden ponds

GREENHOUSES AND
CONSERVATORIES

Everlite Greenhouses, Inc.
9515 Gerwig Lane
Suite 115
Columbia, MD 21046
Tel: (301) 381-3881
*Greenhouses, sunrooms, and
conservatories – catalog available*

Four Seasons Greenhouses
5005 Veterans Memoria
Highway
Holbrook, NY 11741–4516
Tel: (800) 645-9527
*Greenhouses and sunrooms –
catalog available*

**Gardener's Supply
Company**
128 Intervale Road
Burlington, VT 05401
Tel: (800) 688-5510
Free catalog available

Gothic Arch Greenhouses
P.O. Box 1564
Mobile, AL 36633
Tel: (800) 628-4974
*Wooden greenhouses and
supplies, conservatories – catalog
available*

Northwest Eden Sales, Inc.
15103 N.E. 68th Street
Redmond, WA 98052
Tel: (800) 545-3336
*Greenhouses and supplies –
catalog available*

**Pacific Coast Greenhouse
Manufacturing Co.**
8360 Industrial Avenue
Cotati, CA 94931
Tel: (707) 795-2164
*Redwood greenhouses and
sunrooms – catalog available*

Sun Glo Solar Greenhouses
4441-26 West, Dept NGS
Seattle, WA 98199
Tel: (800) 647-0606
Free catalog available

Sun Room Company
322 East Main Street
Leola, PA 17540
Tel: (800) 426-2737
Catalog available

GARDEN STRUCTURES AND
ORNAMENTS

Alsto's Handy Helpers
P.O. Box 1267
Galesburg, IL 61401
Tel: (800) 447-0048
*Cedar patio furniture and swings,
metal lawn chairs, gliders –
catalog available*

Ballard Designs
1670 DeFoor Avenue, NW
Atlanta, GA 30318–7528
Tel: (404) 351-5099
*Cast architectural ornaments,
metal and glass chairs, benches
and tables – catalog available*

Country Casual
17317 Germantown Road
Germantown, MD 20874–
2999
Tel: (301) 540-0040
*Trellises and teak furniture –
catalog available*

French Wyres
P.O. Box 131655
Tyler, TX 75713
Tel: (903) 597-8322
*Trellis, urns, wire plant stands,
and topiary frames – catalog
available*

Garden Accents
4 Union Hill Road
Conshohocken, PA 19428
Tel: (215) 825-5525
*Antique and modern garden
ornaments, statuary, lighting,
stone and metal urns – catalog
available*

Garden Concepts
P.O. Box 241233
Memphis, TN 38124–1233
Tel: (901) 756-1649
*Furniture, structures and
accessories in wood – catalog
available*

Gardener's Eden
P.O. Box 7307
San Francisco, CA 94120–7307
*Garden ornaments, metal, twig
and wicker garden furniture –
catalog available*

MAGAZINES

Flower & Garden
P.O. Box 7507
Red Oak, IA 51566

**Horticulture, The
Magazine of American
Gardening**
P.O. Box 53879
Boulder, CO 80321

Organic Gardening
33 East Minor Street
Emmaus, PA 18098

INDEX

PHOTOGRAPHY CREDITS

Specially commissioned photography © Anness Publishing Limited. All photography by Peter Anderson except as listed below.

Key: t = top; b = bottom; c = centre; l = left; r = right.

Paul Forrester: pages 1; 23 tr; 64 tr, br; 88 br; 137 bl, cb, br; 157. John Freeman: pages 2/3. Michelle Garrett: page 139 tr. Jacqui Hurst: jacket (front flap) b; pages 88 cr; 99 t; 142 tl.

ADDITIONAL PICTURE CREDITS

The publishers would like to thank the following for permission to reproduce images in this book:

Jerry Harpur: jacket (back) tl (designer, Susan Whittington), tr (Anne Alexander-Sinclair), bl (The Dingle, Welshpool), br (designers, Brian Daly and Allan Charman); pages 5 tl, tr (Anne Alexander-Sinclair), bl, br (designers, Brian Daly and Allan Charman); 7 t (Exbury Gardens, Hants), c, b; 8 (designer, Susan Whittington); 9; 11 tl; 28 t (Exbury Gardens, Hants), b; 43 l (Barnsley House, Gloucs), r; 52 (Fudlers Hall, Mashbury); 53 (Anne Alexander-Sinclair); 55 l & br (Park Farm, Chelmsford), tr; 67 t (Marcus Harpur), b (Park Farm, Chelmsford); 75 t (Albert Williams), b (Sticky Wicket); 84 (The Dingle, Welshpool); 85; 91 t (Penny Crawshaw); 117 b (designer, Beth Chatto); 128 (designer, Beth Chatto); 129 (designers, Brian Daly and Allan Charman); 131; 141 bl br.

Peter McHoy: jacket (front flap) t; pages 4; 11 tr, b; 15 tr, cr; 21 bl; 24 br; 26 br; 31 br; 33 br; 35 bl; 37 br; 45 br; 49 tr; 51 tl; 57 cl, bl, br; 59 br; 60 bl; 61 tl, ct, tr, bl, cb; 70 bl; 73 tr; 76 tr; 78 br; 81 br; 82 br; 87 b; 89 br; 92 bl; 93 br; 95 cl, cr, bl, br; 99 bl, br; 100 br; 101 br; 103 t, cl; 105 tr; 108 tl, ct, tr, br; 109 bl; 111 t; 113 cr; 117 t; 122 br; 124 bl; 125 br; 126 b; 135 tl; 136 tr, c; 138 tl, ct, bl, cb, br; 141 t; 143 tl, tr, bl, cb; 145 c; 146 br; 149 b.